the collection

the
collection

Including:
maroc
the viet nam project
the play
sundries

by ron callison

Published by:
Mango Moon Press, Inc.
mangomoonpress.com
info@mangomoonpress.com
mangomoonpress@yahoo.com

First American Edition
Published by Mango Moon Press, Inc.

Printed in the United States of America

the acknowledgments

**for my always encouraging
proof readers:**

pamela callison
colleen graf
karla lingren
orville easterly

and long time friend

loren lingren

thank you

to Pam

the table of contents

the preface
(revised August 5, 2012)

My book has been out a couple of weeks now and the first question I get is "Ron, what's your book about?" It's about people. I have met and spoken with, eaten with, drank with, laughed with, cried with, slept with (well, in the same room), hugged and kissed and been with many people all over the world. The stories that follow are centered on the events with these people. The events that have occurred during these encounters have inspired these stories and my intent in the writing and sharing of them with you is to bring you into the event and draw us all closer together. Please don't read through this book at a sitting. It's not a novel. Each story is meant to stand alone. Read a story, dog ear the page, put the book down and come back another day. Eat the words...slowly.

Ron Callison

P.S. added August 19, 2012

I overheard Pam speaking to our friend Cynthia yesterday about the book. She said, "We're all so busy no one has time to read a book any more but we can read a story. Sit down with a cup of coffee and read one of Ron's stories and then go back to your day." Good idea!

Banned in Viet Nam! The Information Department of Ho Chi Minh City has banned this book.

maroc

preface to maroc

Maroc is French for Morocco. The French and Arabic hybrid that is Morocco makes a unique culture apart from Arabia and Europe–its own place. My wife Pam and I traveled around Europe on a BMW motorcycle and lived in a Moroccan-made pup tent for the year of 1971. This story is an account of a hitchhiking experience we had across the Sahara Desert to El Aauin in the Spanish Sahara. For two kids from the affluent suburbs of the US it was a "true adventure".

chapter one

Rumors were a certainty. We developed our own policy concerning them. If we heard the same rumor twice, it was reassuring. If three times, it became almost fact. Well, at least fact enough to warrant investigation. Such was the rumor concerning travel to the Canary Islands from Morocco.

At this time in history (1971) Morocco and Spain were not on speaking terms, so there was no direct travel connection between the two counties and their territories. Now, the sure way to get to the island paradise was to go back to Spain and ferry over on one of the many tourist boats that worked the route. But from the south of Morocco this looked like an unnecessary backtrack and the Michelin map showed a ferry from the Spanish Sahara to Gran Canaria. But, getting to Aaiun in the Spanish Sahara was a problem. As is the case in many squabbling African counties, the border between Morocco and the Spanish Sahara was in dispute and the token exchange of fire power between border guards threatened the crossing, not to mention the lack of a road across the desert.

This is where the rumor comes in. It seems that the border dispute was not heated enough to thwart trade between the two countries. Trucks from each would carry goods to the frontier across this corner of the Sahara Desert and exchange them, load for load, right there in the middle of the desert and each would then go its merry way back to its respective country for distribution. We heard that, for a small fee, it was possible to hitchhike on top of these trucks to the frontier and from there drive to Aaiun on the primitive, but at least existent road south.

'We' are Ron and Pam. Products of the baby boom, the Cold War, The Bomb, Hot Rods, Elvis, The Beatles, fashion and fad and all the other influences of the affluent fifties and sixties in suburban America. I had a passion for the automobile (and all things mechanical) and naturally chose one of the symbols of the modern, industrial age for our transportation in Europe--a BMW motorcycle. The machine lived up to its reputation and proved a worthy transport and faithful friend. Pam was a much more cerebral, well read, individualistic thinker than myself and the genesis of our ideas originated with her but I had the ability to expand and act on them. She was the theorist--I the implementor. We had a oneness of mind that resulted from the cohesiveness of the protest era of the late sixties among the youth. This was before the drugs and violence wiped out the idealism of the era. It was a short time in history, this idealistic period, but one that left a mark for decades. After our four years of marriage and a gallant (and successful) effort toward the 'American Dream' it was time to cash in the chips and head East.

chapter two

We wintered in Marrakech at the beckoning of Crosby, Stills and Nash after a freezing, nine day ride south from Luxembourg. It was here that we began our study of life experienced by other peoples, living in other places. This study was to take us to all four corners of Europe and Great Britain over a year's time, living in a pup tent and traveling on the bike. We took a side trip during our winter hibernation over the Atlas Mountains to the village of Zagora on the edge of the Sahara Desert and lazed in the sun and the market places for a couple of weeks before deciding it was time to follow up on the rumor and head for the legendary Canary Islands, Columbus' first stop on his way to destiny (but for us, a sun soaked beach, escaping the culture that evolved from his momentous voyage). For we were two of the drop out generation, spoiled brats, throwing tantrums on the streets of America--in search of something (of what we did not know) but mostly escaping the disillusionment of what we did know. We thought we knew what was wrong with our society (the Viet Nam War, materialism, mindless work, voyeuristic sports and entertainment to name a few) but we had no answers to solve the problems, and travel to these other cultures seemed part of the learning process to find those answers. Could we find, in these other societies, what we thought was missing in ours?

Tony and Sherry also had a BMW and upon our meeting in Agadir decided to attempt the adventure across the desert together. Tony and Sherry had been to Woodstock so this gave them credentials as certified, card carrying hippies.

There was a certain awe on my part concerning this fact as Woodstock represented the reality, or maybe the realization of the dream of the time. Of course, Altamont, later that same year, represented the death of this dream, never to be resurrected. Tony and Sherry had much less of the idealism we so arrogantly possessed and were mostly just out for 'kicks' so our only real attraction to each other was the bikes. The security, that increased numbers provides, made traveling together palatable and it would only be for a short time anyway.

We were aware of the camel market in Goulimeme and made that our first stop heading south. After an early start, we rolled into the desert village amidst much dust and activity. We missed most of the camel auction but caught enough to get the flavor of the beasts and their masters. The camel, to us, was the symbol of this culture. One cannot get a feel for the animal's character behind the fence of a zoo; consequently, Westerners have little respect for the attributes (both negative and positive) of this creature. Upon entering Morocco from Ceuta the camel was our first visual assault. It was yoked with a cow, plowing a field followed by a djellaba clothed farmer, whipping and coercing the pair along. Now, for a couple of pampered city kids, this was the beginning of culture shock. The temper and obstinateness of this animal is very similar to the character of these rugged people. I wonder who got it from whom.

After several hours of walking around the market and village, taking in the sights and sounds and smells of an Arab market day we left for Tan-Tan, the last village before the desert and the beginning of the truck caravan to the frontier. Upon our arrival we were greeted by the sight of our prospective transportation--the ubiquitous Ford 2 ½ ton stake side truck. This vehicle is the backbone of Moroccan freight transportation. They are the smelly, road hogging, lumbering mechanical beasts of burden accommodating the industry of the country. They are both loved and despised by the people--a necessary evil for the transition to the modern age. They represent to the modern age what the camel represents to the ancient. We witnessed many accidents involving these vehicles with shrouded bodies lying along side the road and shocked, pale faced bystanders in attendance. We shuddered at the thought that we were about to participate in this folly. The only consolation was that we knew there would be no traffic to contend with on the desert and euphorically went ahead with our plans.

Tan-Tan is similar to every other rural Moroccan village in layout and architecture. The central square is lined with the businesses of the village and the residential area cowers behind as if not to exist at all. The whitewashed buildings and red tiled roofs give an air of neatness that is overpowered by the dust and diesel fumes of the traffic. The interior of the buildings are all ceramic tile--mostly blue and white. The tile work gives a feeling of stark elegance to the otherwise simple, almost poverty stricken, nature of this rising third world nation. The café is the meeting place for everyone in a Moroccan village. The café is the political soap box, the newspaper, the employment office, the location for the business transactions of a country. Every business pact in the country is made in the village cafes over a cup of steaming hot mint tea poured from silver pots into small glass cups. If one smell could identify Morocco, it would be the smell of mint tea. The mint leaves are placed in the glass cups with much, too much, sugar and the boiling hot water poured over. The taste is pure sugar--the aroma is pure mint--the taste sensation is pure delight.

The four of us took our place at a table, ordered the customary tea and waited to size up the situation. We had always been centers of attraction everywhere we went because of our bikes and never had trouble engaging conversation. The Moroccan police use BMW's and the people love and appreciate the machine for its practical as well as symbolic nature. Because of the people's feelings for the machine, this affection often times overflowed onto us as riders and we were treated with respect and interest. The café patrons saw the bikes upon our arrival and it wasn't long before we were included in their conversations and asked about the bikes and what we were doing in this last outpost of population. We inquired about the truck caravan and the possibility of hitching a ride on top and were referred to a driver sitting at one of the tables. He was a young man, about our age, dressed in the attire of a trucker, with black pants, blue shirt and sandals. The truck drivers have an elevated status here and wield an air of authority over the 'common' people. He sat with his co-driver and their young helper and the driver and co-driver of a companion truck. For safety sake the trucks always drove in pairs.

In this remote area it is unusual to find people who speak French (everyone speaking Arabic, of course). French is the second language in most of the urban areas, as Morocco was once a French territory. The French influence is still very prominent and the combining of the Arab and French customs has allowed the emergence of a new culture, with its own uniqueness. To our surprise these drivers spoke French and Spanish as they needed to converse with the Spanish drivers at the frontier. We presented our plan to Mohammed, as he introduced himself, and proceeded to bargain on a price for the ride. Everything in Morocco is negotiated by bargaining. We agreed on 15 durham per person (about three dollars) and then found out that preparations were being made to leave right now. We, also learned that the trip took two and a half days. We later discovered that the fee we paid covered food, too, but since we didn't know this at the time, we rushed to the market before leaving to buy enough food for the trip. We were used to carrying food and cooking utensils as this was our traveling lifestyle anyway so it was no trick for us to do this. The truck was already loaded and all that was left to do was for us to load the bikes and leave. We were thrilled to have found the driver so easily and to have arrived at the price that we thought was very cheap.

The truck on which we were to ride was pulled along side a dock that was about three feet lower than the top of the loaded vehicle. The load was covered with a tarp and we had to muscle the bikes up on top and position each one to the edge of the load. The four of us then simply sprawled out on top of the load with a ring side panorama of the trek ahead. We climbed aboard, with Mohammed driving and his co-diver and young helper in the cab. Our companion truck followed. The sky was the typical crystal blue of all desert skies. It was a good day for adventure!

chapter three

As we drove toward the desert we noticed a Volkswagen bus with a group of non-Arabs following us, but gave little attention to it at the time. However, we made several stops and the VW would stop, also, at a distance, and continue when we continued. We decided that they were following us for the purpose of getting across the desert in the bus. We didn't know at the time if they had made arrangements with Mohammed to pay him for leading them across but found out later that they had not, and this proved to be a major source of irritation for our driver and provided us with some unexpected surprises.

We didn't go far before we stopped in an area where there were many low, scrawny bushes and the helper ran out and started throwing dead branches up on top of the load to us. We were puzzled as to the purpose of this wood but were told to stack it anywhere we could find on top. We later found out it was fire wood for cooking. Further on, we stopped to pick up a Bedouin camel herdsman. He, also, climbed on top of the load with us, the bikes and the firewood and sat in the corner surveying the country side and paying no attention to us. This man was very regal in appearance. He wore a dark purple djellaba with a white shirt. He had the usual Arab mustache but otherwise clean shaven face. He was very handsome and sat with an air of pride and self assurance. He was probably on his way to his camp from the market.

Our next stop was for water. The water was drawn from a pit at the end of a large concrete slab about 50' by 30'. The slab sloped toward the pit for the purpose of collecting rain and dew. My thought was that this must have been a government sponsored project for the trucks that plied this trade route as the whole water collection system was new and very clean.

So far on the trip we had not gone over about 25 miles per hour and this was to be top speed for the entire trip, with most traveling being done at an even slower pace. The terrain became more barren and more rocky. We then came to one of the most dramatic sights of terrain we had ever seen. We arrived upon the banks of an ancient river bed–the River Draa. We could see to the other side of this great canyon through which this once mighty river flowed. It was easy to imagine the rushing water before us and could fantasize about the water parting to allow our crossing like the Israelites escaping Pharaoh. We proceeded to ford the invisible waterway. The truck wound down a rough track on the side of the bank, passing boulders as big as the truck itself. The deep gashes made by the flow of the water of another millennia presented great obstacles to this machine of the present millennia. The driver was very careful and very slow, traveling at a crawl. Every movement of the truck on the rough terrain was magnified toward the top of the load where we sat, giving us the feeling of sailors atop the main mast of a schooner in a gale. This carnival ride down the river bank was very intimidating. We were sure the truck would tip over any moment and all of those mental pictures of the truck accidents we had accumulated in our minds in the past months came flooding back to us. We imagined our own shrouded bodies lying beside the overturned beast, bested by nature's hand and man's incompetence. In time we became numb to the potential danger and were able to thoroughly enjoy the tremendous view we had of this dried river bed. We could imagine the flowing water over these huge rocks and wondered what the land around it looked like before the desert laid claim to it. We reached the bottom of the bank and drove for a short time on the floor of the river itself, looking up at both sides, feeling the water flow over us. We started up the other side and eventually out. We had only been on the truck a couple of hours and already we had our money's worth!

chapter four

Travel South from the river bed led to a more stereotypical 'desert' terrain of rolling sand dunes. The rippling sand rolled toward us in great waves as our truck ascended and descended each swell, like a dingy in the vast expanse of the Atlantic. It's this sand that makes the trip across the desert uncertain in that the winds move the sand over any existing tracks and leave only new sand dunes in their place. The track follows the coast line; even though, we never saw the ocean, but one could probably veer too far east into the great unknown of the Sahara and never be heard from again. Also, the sand presents problems for the trucks getting stuck. This is where the helper earns his keep (besides cooking). Each truck is equipped with a pair of track grids that were used on desert aircraft landing fields in World War II. When stuck, if the helper couldn't simply dig out, then he put the tracks under the tires which allowed the truck to move ahead the length of the track. We never required the tracks but we were in constant need of being dug out. The going was very slow during this digging out period (not that we were speedy at any time).

The VW bus was still tagging along having less difficulty than the truck through the river bed but equal difficulty in the sand. There were at least four people in the bus and rather than dig, the passengers would get out and push. The presence of the bus became more and more of an annoyance to Mohammed. His frustration level would escalate when we got stuck and the bus gained ground on us. When the bus got stuck he cheered and tried even harder to 'lose' them. The fact that the bus was able to keep up was a real attack on his pride both as driver and 'adventurer' in this wilderness arena. We perceived all of this information about the driver's attitude toward the VW from body language and gestures toward the pesky irritation, interspersed with the word 'Volkswagen' in the blur of Arabic words. We began to see the resentment well up in him at the presence of this bane of his existence but had no idea yet what the consequences of this resentment would be.

After about an hour, in the midst of this sea of sand, we stopped for no apparent reason. Our hitchhiking Bedouin descended from the truck, extended parting gratitudes with the men in the cab, and proceeded to walk off toward the horizon. There were no apparent landmarks visible (at least to us desert greenhorns) but his camp must have been over 'yonder'. This event amazed us all in many ways. First, how did they all know this was were his camp was as a 360 degree vista revealed pure sand? Secondly, what did his animals eat out in this remote region? Also, what must life be like living many miles from the closest population center and serviced only by trading trucks at infrequent intervals? His lifestyle could both be envied and abhorred. Was he really missing anything living away from the great cities?

Not much after the departure of our fellow hitchhiker we witnessed the unfolding of a natural drama. We came upon a small herd of camels. (The herdsman was certainly near but not in our sight.) There were three or four adult animals and a calf walking with its mother. We were traveling at our usual snail's pace, parallel to their path. The mother and the baby came to a dune where they had a choice of taking the high road or the low road and the mother took the high road. The baby, probably not even aware that a decision on direction had to be made, took the low road simply because that is were it was headed. After about a hundred yards or more the baby realized that Mother was way up on the hill and he was way down here. The dune was too steep for the baby to climb and panic overtook him at once. He let out a mournful braying sound of distress to alert Mom to his predicament and the adult animal looked down with patient, motherly chagrin at the misguided youth and proceeded to communicate with him in camel lowings. She was telling him to go back to the place where the elevation of the land changed and take the high road to meet her up above. The baby paced back and forth several times, uncertain of which way to go, becoming more panicked all the time. Finally the mother started walking back toward the separation point to lead her baby. The baby followed, braying all the way, and finally met Mom at the intersection. The appreciation on the baby's part was evident and the mother licked it on the face and neck in typical bovine fashion and the two of them headed off together on the high road to catch up with the others in the herd. The baby kicked up its heels joyfully like a gymnast practicing the routines and followed Mom closely like the tail must follow the creature. This whole episode took about fifteen minutes as we drove along side of them. It was something straight out of National Geographic! Who needs TV!

chapter five

Evening was approaching and it was time to stop for camp. The two trucks pulled along side each other and the helper set about building a fire and preparing dinner. The VW parked a good ways off but still in sight. Mohammed and the other driver and co-drivers sat around the camp fire talking about the VW, waiting for the first pot of water to boil for the ubiquitous mint tea. We were invited to join them around the fire, of course, and were interested in the conversation concerning the unwanted 'guest'. The subject was momentarily dropped when dinner was ready and to our delight there was enough prepared for us, too.

Now, we thought we had been eating pretty good on the road with our camp stove meals but what was prepared for us tonight ranked with any four star restaurant. The dish was the traditional Moroccan Tajeen. Moroccan food is served in a central bowl with the diners sitting around cross legged (on the floor) and dipping into the single bowl. Each person breaks off a hunk of bread from the main loaf and then breaks off small pieces from the hunk and dips them into the main food bowl and scoops out the food and juice on the bread. Tajeen is a stew made of meat, potatoes, turnips, carrots and other vegetables for variation. The helper claimed the meat was camel but it could have been donkey or goat. The spices are what make this dish truly Moroccan. They use saffron and paprika, giving the dish a colorful, golden look as well as a good taste. This simple meal was truly the best dinner any of us had eaten since we had been on the road. After dinner we leaned back to enjoy the after-dinner mint tea and conversation around the fire.

To our surprise, Mohammed produced a bottle of whiskey! He didn't offer any to us or the co-drivers and the driver of the companion truck drank only a little but Mohammed drank to excess. This use of alcohol is very rare in the Arab nations as it is strictly forbidden by the Koran. Users are looked down upon by most citizens and regarded with disdain. Mohammed was certainly not accustomed to heavy drinking as it didn't take much to make him drunk and with the drunkenness came a personality change that provided a new twist in the desert adventure. He became more hateful toward the VW and the people who were essentially stealing from him right in front of his eyes. It was easy to sympathize with him and share in his disgust of the leaches. In the blur of the Arabic words the word 'Volkswagen' was spat out of his mouth with the uttermost contempt. He became more boisterous and eventually smashed the glass cup from which he was drinking with a tire iron from the truck. This event naturally put us on edge and to make matters worse his wrath was now directed at us, as the silent bus, silhouetted on the far away dune, mocking his manhood, failed to respond to his tirade. His companions momentarily calmed him down and it was time to turn in for the night. The four of us spread our sleeping bags out on the ground, climbed in, and apprehensively attempted sleep, thinking the episode was over.

We were down only for a short time when Mohammed started ordering everyone to get on the truck, for we were leaving, now! He had decided that the best way to lose the VW was to drive off in the night, with the lights off, so they could not follow. We had no choice but to obey. We hastily rolled our bags and climbed aboard our mechanical ship of the desert with our very own Captain Ahab at the helm. The preview of fear that accompanied the smashing of the glass earlier came flooding over us all with full force now. If Mohammed's companions were of the same mind as he, then we were certainly at a disadvantage. If he were the only 'crazy' one, then Tony and I could have handled him alone easily. The fear that overtook us was more of the unknown than of anything we could put our finger on.

The motors roared to life from their evening slumber and jerkingly propelled their cargo and hapless crews into the pitch of the night. We continued our ascent and descent on the waves of sand without the advantage of visual perspective. Each new rising was a surprise sensation followed by the expected fall and subsequent rise again. The night was black and moonless and the multitude of stars provided little light for the advancing armada of two. Certainly there was nothing to run into out here in this great expanse of sand and we were not going far enough to get lost and Mohammed probably couldn't get lost out here anyway but we were just not sure what he was up to. We drove for about twenty minutes, stopped, and we were told that this was were we were going to sleep, and the melee ceased as abruptly as it had begun. We confusedly climbed down off the truck, unrolled our bags and tried to go to sleep again.

chapter six

Pam, Sherry, Tony and all of the truck personnel fell asleep very soon after the excitement of the evening wore off. I, on the other hand, could not get comfortable sleeping with the fear of this drunken trucker hanging over me. I became the self appointed night watchman for our small band of pilgrims. To my own surprise, I was so uncomfortable with the situation that I took my Swiss Army knife from my bag, opened it, and slid it up the sleeve of my coat while lying in my bag pretending to sleep, but eyes wide open. The thought of having to use the knife as a weapon of self defense was abhorrent to me. After all, this violent nature was one of the things that our idealism rebelled against in our native culture and I was ashamed that I was now exhibiting that same violent nature which I detested. I tried to rationalize the self defense aspect of my aggression but when I thought of having to plunge the steel blade into another soul's body I convulsed in disgust.

We were positioned such that I could oversee the trucks and every person, as well as the route over which we had just traversed. I laid there ruminating my thoughts like a cow in pasture and waited. In about an hour, or was it three, four, time was irrelevant, I saw a faint glow of a light on the horizon. It wasn't sunrise, no, it wasn't a morning glow. This was an electric light glow. It disappeared. It was black again. Minutes later it appeared again, then disappeared. Was the desert night playing tricks on my fatigued mind like it does with a mirage during the day, to trick the mind into seeing a body of water? I realized this possibility and was prepared to laugh at myself for being caught in the trap of illusion. But this was no illusion! There was a light coming toward us from the distance and the appearing and disappearing was the light rising and falling on the swells of the sand dunes. There was a vehicle coming our way!

As the light danced toward us, the intensity kept increasing against the black background of the night sky. It was like one of the stars was on a collision course with our camp. It became so bright that I knew it was just over the next dune and would burst upon us any second, blinding us with its searing light. The desert air was so clear that there were no obstacles to the rays of light. The light continued its appearing and disappearing act for a long, long time. Wild possibilities rushed through my mine. Wild swings of emotion flooded my being. Fear. Dread. Desperation. Expectation. Deliverance. Salvation. And, like the ancient Greeks with all of their gods, I erected one shrine to the god that may have been forgotten--The Unknown! The drama was intense and I was a solitary audience!

chapter seven

The advancing light was so slow in coming I had
lots of time to ponder its source. Was it the VW?
I dismissed this immediately as impossible for it
would be sure suicide for them to have moved in
the black of night with no knowledge of direction.
Was it another trading truck as we were certainly
on the track south and it would seem reasonable
to encounter other trucks heading for the frontier?
I supposed this would be possible but why would
they be traveling at night? It was winter in the
Sahara and the pleasantly mild days presented
no problems in overheating the trucks so night
driving to take advantage of the coolness would
be unnecessary. Were they desert raiders? I
knew the very top of our load contained
vegetables, grown in the temperate, fertile
regions of Morocco, not a very likely booty, but
what else may have been under the vegetables?
We were in a relatively lawless sector, especially
considering the border dispute in progress.
'Desert raiders' was elevated to the top of my list
of visitors coming our way. No matter who was
coming there was nothing I could do to stop them.
I woke Pam, Sherry, and Tony and pointed out
the coming light without showing my alarm.
Waking from a sleep, they had not had all the
time I did to conjure up movie scenes of death
and destruction so we all decided the best thing
to do was just wait.

The light was now close enough to be
accompanied by the sound of the vehicle. At the
pinnacle of the dunes the angry roar of the engine
announced its presence. As the vehicle plunged
down into the canyon between summits the roar

was muffled almost to a purr. The light became blindingly bright when we could see the actual source of it at the peak of the dunes and finally it crested the last dune and bore down on us like accusing eyes to inspect our darkest deeds. The eyes of light stopped close to camp. The idling motor silenced. The vehicle was a Ford stake side just like ours. Men exited the machine. Mohammed and his comrades were up and walking toward the intruder in the now darkened scene. They portrayed no sense of alarm. One of the men from the newly arrived vehicle had a flashlight. Its light flitted about like a firefly on a Midwestern eve and the Arabic language began to flow from all players on the stage. The flashing light revealed that its owner was wearing a uniform! I could see the 'X' of leather belts across his chest like so many police and military uniforms I'd seen. He wore a brimmed hat that was police-like. They were, in fact, the police!

As malcontent protestors of the unsettled times of the late sixties, we were the least likely people to welcome the police. But, welcome them we did. Oh, not verbally, but in our hearts and between ourselves we were glad to see them. The thought never entered our minds that we might be the object of this police intervention and were glad to see that this drunken trucker got caught in his folly. The policemen never once spoke to us. After a short conversation between the drivers and police they all dispersed to their own vehicles and Mohammed came to us and told us to get on the truck, we were leaving again. We were completely clueless as to what had transpired and what was ahead, but, again, had no choice but to obey. We drove only for a short time. All three trucks stopped and we were told that we would spend the rest of the night here. The police truck continued on and after only moments it disappeared completely. How strange it was to me to realize how fast it had vanished after the great length of time it took to appear. For the third time we unrolled our bags and finished our night's rest, confused at what had transpired and what lay ahead, but comforted that danger had spared us.

chapter eight

Morning greeted us with grey skies, a cool, almost cold, wind and somber Arab chaperones. There was a general mood of melancholy amongst everyone and little conversation. After the usual European style continental breakfast of bread and coffee, we loaded up and continued on the voyage south.

The terrain became less sandy and more hard surfaced but still not a single leaf of vegetation. The undulations of the dunes ceased but were replaced by rocks. The going was still slow and proceeded without incident or interest for the rest of the day. In the late afternoon we arrived at Tarafaya. Tarafaya is a military outpost just north of the frontier and very close to the Atlantic Ocean. It consisted of two rows of primitive buildings and was occupied by a rag-tag bunch of Moroccan troops. We saw the police truck parked there that had overtaken us the night before and upon arrival Mohammed and the other driver disappeared into one of the buildings behind the truck. He came out later even more dejected than when he went in and with little conversation, dinner was prepared and we were ushered to one of the buildings to sleep on cots. During the night we heard several reports of gunfire in the distance. I think those soldiers had to justify there existence in that place and firing a few rounds now and again kept everyone on their toes.

We never learned what got him in trouble. He was certainly in trouble. His mood changed from the arrogant, cocky, respected truck driver of a government trade vehicle to a beaten puppy with its tail between its legs. Did he get in trouble for taking hitchhikers (us) across the desert? Did he get in trouble for driving at night? Maybe there are safety rules concerning night driving. Did it have something to do with the VW bus? We never saw the bus again but can only assume they made it. The trip was not at all impossible for that vehicle as long as they didn't get lost. The mystery of the evening and the outcome for the players added to the adventure of the trip.

The next morning we arose to another grey day (which seemed fitting), loaded up, and drove for a few hours till we could see a row of trucks in the distance. They were all parked with their rear ends toward us and the contents of their load lying on the ground next to the truck. Upon our arrival we each backed up to a truck, muscled the bikes off, and the exchange of goods was accomplished.

Morocco 1971

the viet nam project

preface to the viet nam project

On February 3, 1994 the Clinton administration lifted the 19 year trade embargo on Viet Nam. When I tell the story I always say "I took the next plane out of town." In reality it took me until April to get my arrangements made and go. I was still one of the first Americans to go to Viet Nam to do business (aside from the mega corporations). My intent was to build a Bromeliad nursery and grow the plants for local sale and maybe export. Now, after 18 years and lots of good travels I present you with a few stories documenting this project.

A word about the Vietnamese language:

Vietnamese is a mono-syllabic language. Westerners "anglicized" the language by combining syllables; hence Viet Nam became Vietnam, Ha Noi became Hanoi. I have used the mono syllabic spellings in these stories in keeping with their language.

the rain (for Be Chi)

It's raining right now, a heavy, good rain. But she
doesn't like the rain. She doesn't like to wear a
rain coat either so we head for the nearest
building, the Post Office, to wait it out. She parks
the motorcycle while I carry the things we just
bought at the market into the building. Waiting, I
see her walking toward me across the wide
sidewalk between the parking area and the
building. She's carrying her hat, which she just
removed and is shaking the new rain from her
close-cropped black hair, glad to be close to
shelter. How could she live here all her life and
not like the rain? But maybe that's exactly why
she doesn't like the rain. The rain is somehow the
great equalizer here. Everyone is rained on, the
rich, the poor, foreigners, beggars, aristocrats--
everyone. But, of course, she isn't "everyone."
She isn't one of them. She's very different. Oh
sure, the family has aristocratic origins and she
carries herself like a true aristocrat, not in a
snobbish or aloof way, no, not at all, but in a way
that commands respect from people and they
don't even know why they should respect her, but
they just know they should, so they do. But she
still doesn't like the rain.

We sit at a long, dark wooden bench with a high
back. The heavy rain outside draws my attention
like a moth to the flame and holds it for some
time. She doesn't watch the rain. She sits
quietly, mostly thinking to herself, looking around
occasionally, but mostly quietly thinking. I break

my fixed gaze from the rain and turn to her to exchange light conversation. I know she isn't happy about having to wait out the rain and I think conversation will relieve her a little. She speaks softly, like she always does, so softly I have trouble even hearing her sometimes. Aristocrats don't speak loudly. They don't need to. Her English language skill is just like she is, precise, distinct, no frills, but accurate, though simple, like a minimalist drawing. Why cover the whole page when a single line will do?

There were many foreigners in the Post Office, all waiting out the rain, all equalized for the moment. We looked around and tried to decide their nationalities by how they looked. She laughed as she spoke, almost a school girl giggle. French? Russian? Definitely not American. No, I was the only American. I knew that but she couldn't tell. Caucasians all look the same to Asian people. But I could tell because they all don't look the same and for that matter all Asian peoples don't look the same either, but in that Post Office, all of us, a little wet, waiting out the rain, we were all very much the same. All. Maybe that's why she doesn't like the rain.

The rain slowed, very lightly caressing the city after the beating of the heavy downpour, a reassuring caress. The whipping of the downpour was for our own good and not meant to harm us like a father's disciplinary switch on his son's bum giving guidance. I tried to get her to go, but no, she wanted to wait a few more minutes until it stopped completely. Yes, of course, when you don't like the rain even a little bit of it can be a discomfort. We waited. It didn't take long. It never does here. The rain comes and goes quickly. It arrives to work, does its job, and goes home. She tied her hat on as we walked to the parking area. The rain had stopped and she was no longer equalized by it. The aristocrat emerged. As we rode, I caught people looking at us, first at me because I'm a foreigner, but then their eyes were drawn to her and then locked. She's one of them but why is she somehow different? Maybe it's because she doesn't like the rain.

Ho Chi Minh City
August 26, 1994

the motorcycle

Wendell Woon arrived on the afternoon flight from Kuala Lumpur. To meet him at the airport I held a sign with his name. We greeted and introduced ourselves to each other and I took him by taxi to the Sai Gon Omni. Dropping him, I told him I'd be back later to take him for dinner and an introduction to my adopted homeland of Viet Nam. He's a fertilizer broker in Malaysia looking to expand into Viet Nam and needed my help with introductions and guidance around the agricultural community of Ho Chi Minh City. I left him for a couple of hours to settle into his room and returned on my motorcycle to take him around the city a little and then to Kim Long Quan for authentic Hue-style dining. He hesitantly got on the back of the small Honda and off we went. He sat rigidly, not touching my body at all with his. This is a real trick on a small Honda motorcycle. When it came time for our first left turn in traffic, we were almost through it when Wendell broke out into uncontrollable physical nervous-laughter. "So that's how it's done!" I heard his quavering voice in my ear. He just couldn't help himself. He had to laugh. It was his natural body defense-mechanism kicking in to compensate for the nervousness and near terror of the left turn ordeal. His uncontrollable laughter took me back to my first left turn years ago and my own uncontrollable laughter. The irony of laughter as defense against terror still astonishes me to this day.

How does one prepare for riding a motorcycle in Ho Chi Minh City in the post Doi Moi era of the

1990's? Maybe blasting down Fulton Avenue at seventy miles an hour on the Triumph would have been good preparation. Ah, the Triumph, the anti-Christ of motorcycles. The early super bikes of the late sixties were like putting a hand grenade between your legs. With the Triumph, the pin was pulled. I bought it from Jerry Mitchell. He had set it up for T.T. Scrambles. A T. T. Scramble track consists of a dirt road course with at least one jump, usually several, and one high speed flat track 180 degree-left turn. The flat track turn is accomplished at full throttle, full opposite steering lock, bravery, and a small dose of stupidity. The rider's left boot is adorned with a steel-plated sole that is slid on the ground and becomes the real "steering" force in the curve. You would think that a few blasts down Fulton Avenue or a few laps of a T.T. Scramble would be ample preparation for riding a motorcycle in Viet Nam...but maybe not.

Or maybe when we chased a couple of German boys at full tilt on Kawasaki triples in the shadow of the Coliseum in Rome that would be sufficient supplemental preparation. The two boys would dash ahead, throw their heads back in youthful delight, and when they had suitably left us in their dust they would graciously stop and wait for us to catch up. Our BMW was no match for the Kawasakis in this type of competition but let's ride to Nord Cap together and see who fares better. No, Caesar's disapproval not withstanding, the Roman street race was only one more course toward a bachelor's degree in riding a motorcycle in Ho Chi Minh City.

Now I know---England. You have to ride in England to get a feel for driving on "the wrong side of the road." That's it! Now you're in your senior year. Survive a month in England without a head-on and you're ready for a baccalaureate and the streets of Ho Chi Minh City in the 90's. Everything you've learned from the T.T. Scrambles to Fulton Avenue to Rome to "keep left" England all comes together here for the final exam before graduation.

I have dubbed this country the "two wheel country." The primary mode of transport is the Honda 50, and lately 90. If you've ever wondered who really prospered from the horrific human tragedy of the Viet Nam war era, it was Honda. Honda has competitors but Vietnamese people prefer the Honda. It's almost a status symbol. Equal in numbers to the small motorcycles are bicycles and then, in decreasing order of prominence, come the myriad of three-wheeled devices, taxis, a few privately owned cars, and finally trucks and small buses. The "food chain" is determined strictly by size. The largest moving object has the right-of-way and pedestrians look out for themselves.

Traffic negotiation in Viet Nam is like no other place on the planet! It could loosely be described as semi-organized chaos. Traffic flows on the right side of the road but occasions arise where riding on the left side of the street, against the oncoming traffic, is necessary, as in the case of the left turn with Wendell Woon. Another occasion would be if the distance to travel is short. The ride can be made on the left side of the street to avoid crossing the oncoming traffic,

49

slowing the flow, re-crossing the oncoming traffic to make the left turn, and slowing the flow a second time. The ultimate goal of the traffic promenade is to keep moving. Crossing all of the oncoming traffic twice to ride a short distance may slow the traffic more than simply riding on the left side against the oncoming traffic.

The most fascinating phenomenon to me about Viet Nam traffic is the unperturbable composure of the riders and drivers. After five years of intense traffic observation I have only seen one fight and rarely cross words or arguments. For example, when traffic crosses at uncontrolled intersections there seems to be an unwritten law of deference and assertiveness. Each crossing of the intersection demands one or the other of these two disciplines. One time a rider must defer to another, and another time a rider must be assertive and go first. The object, which everyone subconsciously realizes, is for everyone to get through the intersection expeditiously. This is accomplished by deference and assertiveness. If deference to another rider is called for this time, then next time maybe, the situation will call for assertiveness. One time a slight delay. The next time it's made up. Over time it all evens out. To become angry or fretful about who got there first or who has the right of way only slows the process down. Just give and take and all goes well. I find that eye contact is rarely made, also. It seems everyone has a sixth sense for the intersection crossing gambol.

The classic "left turn" illustrates perfectly the concept of "semi-organized chaos." When traveling toward the city center on Nguyen Van

Troi, for example, and deciding to turn left on Huynh Van Banh the rider moves to the extreme left of the traffic flow. Prior to the intersection, assertiveness kicks in and a move to the left into oncoming traffic is required. Any small gap in the oncoming flow presents an opportunity for intrusion. A left turn signal is helpful but many older bikes don't have signals. If the rider has a passenger, the passenger may signal for the rider by extending the left hand with a downward and outward waving action to signify the intent to turn. The time, from the first intrusion into the oncoming flow of traffic, until the left curb is finally met is consumed by asserting and deferring to the oncoming bikes. The oncoming flow sees the left turner ahead and adjusts its speed and direction to either allow the turner to pass in front or behind. If all has gone well the timing of reaching the left curb and reaching the intersection coincide and the turn is completed.

It's important to remember that speeds on the streets are slow at best. The "dance" of the left turn takes place very slowly with ample time for braking to allow for minor indiscretions in technique. Add to the slow speed the unperturbable nature of the riders and the left turn becomes much less daunting. It almost becomes logical, making the modern day left turn lane and left turn arrow of Western traffic control obsolete even before they are introduced.

Ho Chi Minh City
February 1998

the guard (for Sara)

Vod Ka woke first, his alarm sound waking me. I instinctively bolt to my feet sounding my own alarm in the direction of the commotion coming from the gate. I see the darkened figures silhouetted in the night and increase my alarm as I see the man-hands on the gate. Suddenly I realize it's the white-faced man and he's calling my name. I plunge my nose into his hand through the wire of the gate and inhale the foreign aroma he emits. I immediately tell Vod Ka that the white-faced man is a friend. He's been here many times before, with long absences in between, as he stops his alarming. The brown-skinned man opens the gate and they enter. I push my nose into the white-faced man's hands and legs and greedily suck in the smells of his body. I don't jump up on him, remembering he doesn't like that. Vod Ka does and the white-faced man strikes him on the nose and speaks harshly with strange words that are stern and demanding.

I remember the white-faced man from my youth. I would run at the feet of Luc Ky and nip at his neck and pester him until he nipped me back a painful snap. The white-faced man always stroked my head and throat differently than the brown-faced people in the house and he always spoke in gibberish that Luc Ky and I never understood. Luc Ky was the one who introduced me to the white-faced man's kindness. He told me how the strange man had been coming to the house since he himself was a youth and that the white-faced man always treated him with kindness. This information comforted me in the beginning as I learned to know the stranger in spite of the gibberish words he spoke. Luc Ky has long since died but the memory of the white-faced man lives on and now he is here again and it's my turn to introduce him to Vod Ka.

The white-faced man sleeps in a room of his own. In the morning when I arise and am allowed to enter the main house I run straight to the white-faced man's room, stopping at the doorway. I see he is still sleeping. I look around for the young brown-faced girl who always torments me. If I see her, I remain. If she's absent, I walk softly into the room over to the white-faced man, bury my nose into the pit of his arm and thirstily drink in the strange odor of his body. His odor is not bad, not good, just different from the brown-faced people in the house like the difference between two fruits, both uniquely their own but both familiarly manlike. He awakes and reaches over to pull me into his side and I further bury my whole head into the cradle of his body. In ecstacy I murmur low sounds as he strokes my neck and head and throat and nose, caressing in a way the brown-faced men never do. Suddenly the young brown-faced girl appears as if out of a nightmare, barking her harsh words at me to leave the room. I jump up and dash out the corner of the door, narrowly escaping her swinging hand destined for my backside. I dive under the table, momentarily free of her torment.

The white-faced man stays for several days, leaving in the morning of each day, coming home in the middle, leaving again, and coming home again at night. I always greet him at the gate and he greets me only after speaking some gibberish to the brown-faced people in the house. They seem to understand his nonsense-talk but to me it is impossible. I only understand the kind tone he uses with the soft stroke of his hands on my body. He is a welcome respite from the sometimes cruelty of the brown-faced people, especially the young brown-faced girl who never lets me rest. One day the white-faced man returned home with a different smell on his body. He'd been with a stranger! Vod Ka and I sniffed the white-faced man's body intently to determine the origin of this stranger he had been with. Jealousy welled up inside me and I realized maybe he had been sharing his affections with another. I wanted to turn and reject this unfaithful lover but the sudden stroke of his now familiar hand on my neck caressed away all feelings of betrayal and I dismissed the strange intruder as an imposter.

Finally, one day the white-faced man was lying in his room in the afternoon, reading. The young brown-faced girl was nowhere to be seen. I crawled in and laid next to the white-faced man's feet. He continued to read but reached his hand down to stroke my head as he had done so many times in the past. Suddenly I realized this was the last day I would see the white-faced man. No one told me, I just knew. I became somber and began to miss his stroke already so I laid my head on his feet and basked in the comfort of his touch. I became so comfortable I fell asleep. I felt my body twitch and my legs "run." Maybe I was chasing a robber away from the white-faced man and forever endearing him to my debt as his protector. My mind raced in fantasy as I protected the white-faced man from all sorts of evils and I emerged victorious each time and found myself enthroned at the right hand of the white-faced man and the young brown-faced girl was my servant and did everything I said and stroked my head as the white-faced man had taught her. I was awakened from this deep fantasy slumber by the shriek of the young brown-faced girl's voice piercing my ears and my muscles jerked to attention and bolted my body out the door and under the table.

That night the white-faced man and the brown-faced man put big boxes in the noisy machine that slept near the gate. They got inside the noisy machine with the boxes and the noise became louder as the machine moved out the gate. He was gone. I knew forever. I walked back to the room where he slept and took one last lung-full of the sweet foreign aroma and held it deep inside me thinking that it could bring him back to stroke my body again. I exhaled in despair and walked over to lie next to Vod Ka and resume my sentry duties.

Ho Chi Minh City, Viet Nam
October 26, 1999

the haircut

It's the simple things in life that bind us together in our humanity. Cultures conjure up complexities and traditions and procedures and protocols that complicate life, often unnecessarily. The simple things, those which we all do as humans, regardless of culture, race, social or economic status, are what tie us together like sheaves of grain standing in a freshly cut field. These things validate our lineage back to one couple....from one bone of rib....from one lump of clay....from one Creator. Such....is the haircut.

Now, my point of reference here is NOT the unisex Super Cuts/Great Clips hair salons of "modern, civilized, and enlightened society." No, my reference is the Barber Shop....a place for the manly man to have manly needs met without the intrusion of women. The traditional barber shop has a long history of diverse activities above and beyond the simple haircut from doctoring and dentist-ing to political, economic and social hypothesizing and commentary and just general gossip and conversation. The barber shop in Viet Nam is all of this and more.

Thinh, Be and I had returned from Cho Binh Thanh and downtown Sai Gon with time to spare before lunch so off to the Hot Toc for a haircut. We walked a short distance from Ong Cat's house to a shop on Huynh Van Banh and a waiting barber. The traditional "how do you want it cut" conversation took place and then the draping of the torso with the sheet like a sculptor drapes his unfinished masterpiece between work sessions. The craftsman used the common tools of the trade, the scissors, the comb, the skilled hands. The familiar sounds of the clip, clip, clip brought comfort and solace, knowing that the artist was at work, transforming the sow's ear into a silk purse. There is something comforting about the feel of the comb and the scissors and the hands on the head that is seductive and sensual. Now don't jump to conclusions you sex-crazed Americans. I don't mean sensual in the sexual sense. I mean it in the sense that here is an activity that, by its simplicity, relaxes and soothes the entire soul and body into a near-Nirvana state of euphoria.

After completing the trim around the ears and the tapering up the sides and back the construction worker of beauty produced a hand-operated clipper. It had a handle with scissor type grips for the fingers which operated a clipper head about the width of two fingers. He used this tool to shape the exterior of the bouffant he had previously roughed out with the scissors and mowed down wild tentacles of hair like those dandelion stems that grow up in the dichondra. I asked him to use this tool on the bare top of my head because I perceived he wouldn't from the lack of anything there to mow. But, of course, even in a desert of desolation there are always a few bits of vegetation that beat the odds and spring to life to defy and punctuate the bleak landscape.

The bulk of the sculpture completed all that remained was the final polish, the shave. The lawn tender turned surgeon. He stepped up to his operating table and with long, skilled, spidery fingers, removed the old blade from the razor to replace it with a new one. For the patient to see the implement of destruction prior to its use sends shudders down the spine and terror through the heart like a child standing in line to get polio shots at school seeing the needle that is about to be thrust into his tender flesh. Terror must surrender to trust at this point. I could only hope his heart contained noble intentions. I was rewarded by my surrender. The new blade glided over the stubble of the field around my ears and the nape of my neck, leaving behind the silky pathway of smooth skin. Again, the sound of the blade scrapping the stumps of hair down to skin level was comforting and with each pass of the blade I ascended to the next level of heaven.

Finally, I asked him to clip the hairs inside my ears, those cursed addendums to aging that youth need not concern themselves. The decibels of the clip, clip, clip sound reached Pete Townsend levels with the close proximity to the auditory drum. Ear-hair clipping completed, I was surprised at what followed. I felt this soft intrusion into the cavity of my ear. I knew immediately what it was as I had seen many Vietnamese barbers do it before but none had tried it on me. He was thrusting a cotton-tipped shaft, much like a Q-Tip, into my ear cavity to massage and clean it. I was instantly transported back to grade school in L.A. growing up in the '50's. We were taught "never put anything smaller than your elbow in your ear." (I never understood why anyone would want to put an elbow in their ear.) I must have learned this lesson well because the dread of deafness flooded over me like an unanticipated breaker while walking in the foam on the beach. However, like eating an embryonic duckling still in the shell or snails or snake or eel or blood of duck I thought "If they can do this, so can I." I heaved caution over the side like a dead body being returned to the sea and allowed the sadistic inquisitor to proceed. Dread turned to ecstasy! The total concentration of my existence became centered on the pleasure of the internal ear massage. He withdrew the cottoned shaft and squeezed my ear together and thumped the backside of my ear funnel like thumping a watermelon in the market. My ecstasy dipped momentarily as he shifted to the other ear and then climbed to even higher levels as the sense of expectation took over. When he was finished, I laid in the chair, a useless mass of yesterday's Jell-O, trying to compose myself.

Thinh and I finished our haircuts about the same time, thanked and paid the barbers, and walked home in a downpour of Roosevelt Dime-sized raindrops.

I think I'll need another haircut tomorrow.

Thanh Pho Ho Chi Minh, Viet Nam
May 2000

the woman

Retrospecting on my more than twenty trips here I
see now the total experience as an ongoing
continuum of vignettes. The most profound of
these vignettes are the ones that last
milliseconds. These are the momentary glances
on the streets where two souls look into each
other's eyes and gaze deep into the very core of
each other's being and, in that moment,
exchange a life time of conversation and
understanding like the nonverbal exchanges
between an old married couple, school day
buddies, or lovers. In that flash of a glance, while
passing on the street, two people communicate
with each other the entire significance of the
human experience. If I could record the images
of these glances on celluloid, I'd become a
celebrated chronicler of the foundations and
progression of human existence, back to Adam,
worthy of the Pulitzer, not because of my
observations but because of the experience
itself----the glance.

This is the story of one of these vignettes, not the
millisecond glance kind, but one lasting long
enough to assemble bones and flesh. Thinh and
I were at the nursery and a woman was in Ong
Ba's garden next to us looking at his roses. She
saw us through the fence and hailed Thinh. The
two of them volleyed a short conversation and it
became apparent to me she was coming over.
We went to the front gate to let her in. She was a
bicycle vendor of decorative plants and a regular
customer of ours. She had fashioned a wooden
platform on the rear of her bicycle to carry plants

and the combination of that platform and her basket on the front made for a rolling showroom of decorative delight. Bicycle vendors like this ply many different goods through the residential streets of the city, singing out as they pass like carni-hawkers on the midway. I realized when I saw her two-wheeled business that she and I were in the same trade, did exactly the same thing to earn our money, kindred spirits. She entered our nursery and she and Thinh went to a table of Guzmania Rondo that contained several budded plants ready for sale. She chose four pots and they carried them to the front of the nursery to wash and prepare for final retail sale. The three of us squatted by the bulbous ceramic water jar and Thinh proceeded to clean the pots and trim the few bad leaves of the plants, all the time carrying on a soft toned, almost whispering, conversation with the woman as if their very speech would wake the plants.

It was at this time, squatted by the water jar like Neanderthal hunter-gatherers slaughtering the day's kill, that I was able to really look at her. She was beautiful! No, no, no, not the actress-movie star beautiful, although she exhibited those qualities. And no, not the hubba-hubba sex goddess beautiful either, although she belied those qualities too. Her beauty was the earth-mother beauty. And no, not the massive, all powerful, rotund earth mother of Lachaise's *Standing Woman* but the sinewy, all bone, muscle and tendon kind of beauty that so represent the women of the Orient. Her body was as hard as the calves of a Sai Gon cyclo driver. She tilted her head back and cocked her conical hat to one side to reveal her triangular shaped head, broad at her forehead and tapering down to a pointed chin intruded half way by a broad nose. Her teeth were big and white and straight and when she smiled they crowded out all of her other features and became the focal point of the portrait that was her face. But her eyes were the most profound. They were a deep, liquid brown, not black, but dark brown. They were so big they filled her eye sockets leaving little room for white. They glycerine-sparkled when she spoke and boog-a-loo danced when she laughed. They weren't just windows into her soul. They were sliding glass doors.

Then I realized it! Here before me was my illustration to answer Karla's question. The day before I came here this time I called Karla to inquire about Loren. Loren had gone to India and he and Karla both were a bit trepedatious about his trip, a little fear of the unknown. During the course of our conversation I was relating my good experiences in Viet Nam to help her be more at ease with her husband in India. I had made the comment that the Vietnamese people were an incredibly clean people in an incredibly dirty country. I had used this phrase for years when speaking about Viet Nam but Karla wouldn't let it pass without elaboration. She demanded to know how this could be possible. I awkwardly tried to explain myself, stumbling from one bad analogy to another like a drunk from one bar to the next. I felt I never was able to fully communicate my meaning in this phrase and hung up from her disappointed with my failure. Now, here before me, was this woman, a living illustration of what I meant by that phrase. I studied her closely. She was incredibly clean! Her bicycle was very old and looked like a refugee from Roseville's Berry Street Mall. The makeshift platform barely served its required purpose. The streets she rode were littered with trash and dust from the waste of human existence. The air she breathed was thick with diesel smoke, leaded gas fumes, factory smoke and the omnipresent dust. The canals she crossed were liquid sewers with a skin of trash-flotsam almost obliterating from sight the ink water underneath. But the woman, ...she was incredibly clean! Her clothes were not new but quite serviceable, like those old jeans and T-shirts that you can't bare to throw away because they're so comfortable and they've come to define you as you. Well, they were her work clothes, but they were spotlessly clean. Her body looked fresh from the shower and this after rooting through the nurseries of Go Vap all morning beefing up her inventory for this afternoon's sales. Her face, her hair, her hands and fingernails, her feet inside open sandals were all Dial-clean, straight out of a commercial. Here was an incredibly clean Vietnamese woman in an incredibly dirty Viet Nam. How do they do it?

Thinh finished his cleaning duties and began to put two pots each into two plastic bags for her to carry. Her hand disappeared into the depths of her pocket to withdraw a 50,000 Dong note and presented it to Thinh with fingers as delicate as an artist's Russian sable brush. She extended her hand toward him with a spidery motion with the note waving from her finger tips like a goodbye handkerchief waving from a dockside well wisher as the cruise ship pulls away. Thinh received the money and carried the plants to her bicycle for her. She took them, placed them in the basket, eased the stand up and, after a soft adieu, silently glided off down the street like a young boy's toy sail boat glides across a pond. The vignette had ended but the impact lives on.

Ho Chi Minh City, Viet Nam
May 2000

the palace

The sky began to darken and the wind began to blow like a pre-tornado Chicago gale. We bid goodbye to Phoung and pointed the Hon Da toward "The Palace." We had no sooner woven our way into the tight fabric of the five o'clock Sai Gon traffic than the torrent began. The god was angry....or playfully cruel. He threw lightning bolts down like sparks from a bench grinder and then growled with instant, deafening thunder. The rain sounded like a standing ovation. Crack! with lightning. Growl! with thunder. Applause! with rain. Crack! Growl! Applause! Crack! Crack! Growl! Applause! The light/sound show went on and on and the rain fell on our tender faces like stinging buckshot from a 4/10. Crack! Growl! Applause! Sting! Of course, by now we were soaked to the skin. The raincoat was a mockery of protection, an imposter of a facade over a drenched interior. The torrent was a welcome cooling. Oh, I love the rain!

"Turn right here" I directed. "At the next light turn left." It was my final exam for learning the way from Phu Nhuan to "The Palace." We arrived. I passed. My good sense of direction and good memory allowed me to learn the turns in the labyrinth in fewer days than I expected and now I could get home safely. I can now go out alone without calling out the National Guard to retrieve me. Finally, I'm paroled from the prison of dependence.

Be and Thinh have dubbed their new home "The Thousand Star Hotel" as you can stand on the balcony outside their bedroom and look up to a thousand stars. I have dubbed it "The Palace!" This house is beyond any wildest expectations you could have for a house in Viet Nam (or anywhere for that matter!). Hung and Ha collaborated on the design and Khoi supervised the construction. (Khoi is supervising the construction of Toa's house in Da Lat also.) The Palace is three levels. After entering the front gate from the street you cross the parking area for the car and then a tiled outside patio. Passing through a wall of glass doors you enter the high-ceilinged living room with the TV/entertainment center and couch and sitting area and computer table at the back. At the end of the living room you climb a short staircase to the kitchen and dinning area. Out the back door of the kitchen are the water tank and washing area for the kitchen (this is Co Thuy's "office.") From the kitchen you go up another short flight of stairs to the three bedrooms. The one closest the street (over the living room) is Be and Thinh's with the aforementioned star gazing balcony. The rear room over the kitchen is Bo's room with a rear balcony over the kitchen washing area. The middle bedroom is the guest room which they always call my room. They claim to have built this room just for me. I have a window overlooking the field next to the house with cows and water buffalo and ducks grazing in the daytime and frogs croaking at night (the night is full of "night sounds" here as it's out in the country. (This is "The 'burbs of Ho Chi Minh City.") The outside of the house is painted a soft sand color and the inside is a soft pink with dark brown patterned tile floors. The inside is accented with milk chocolate colored moldings and natural wood stair cases. There are two bathrooms, one next to the kitchen and one between my room and Bo's room. They are DELUXE with all of the necessary amenities! When one considers the rooms this family lived in for twenty years at Be's mother's house this place is like a dream come true. I can't imagine how happy they must be living here. The only problem is that it is a little drive to get here from city center.

This land is one of three parcels, two of which were purchased by Toa and Dinh and in the future they will build another house for themselves. (Their current house will be taken for some city expansion project in the future---right of eminent domain.) These two remaining parcels measure 10 meters by 20 meters (200 square meters) that we will fence and cover with shade cloth and Be and Co Thuy will operate a small Bromeliad nursery until Toa and Dinh build their house (the Vuon Lan My Ha Annex!) This place is so quiet and peaceful. There are some distant low sounds of construction as new houses are going up all around here but other than that it's country-quiet.

The phone's been dead for two days so I haven't received any e-mail. Ahhh, it's a fragile place. But what a place to be technologically shipwrecked! I'm living in the lap of luxury in "The Palace" with the best food in the Northern hemisphere (or any hemisphere for that matter!) Be's cooking is exceeding her work at her

Mother's. Now that she's out of her Mother's house she's become the matriarch of her own family. She's ascended to the next level of the social hierarchy and is reveling in her new found position.

After dinner we all sat in the living room to watch TV. "It's Ho Chi Minh's birthday tomorrow" said Thinh. "Oh, that's why all the stations have only communist stuff" I replied. Be laughed with disdainful understanding and said "Yes." Every channel had speeches about Ho and songs about Ho and old movie clips of the war and mass gatherings with Uncle Ho speaking. Thinh looked at me and said "Do you do this for Lincoln or Jefferson?" I spit back a thoughtless, self-righteous "Never!" Before the "r" of the word had escaped my mouth, I tried in vain to suck the whole word back in. With awkward back peddling I said "Well, we put their pictures on our money." "And their birthdays are holidays" I added. The more I watched the propaganda machine in action the more I thought how well oiled our own machine was. In fact it functions so well we can't even see the parallels that exist here and even deny it's existence. It's all just patriotic, nationalistic bullshit! It tears peoples apart by emphasizing the differences rather than drawing peoples together by emphasizing the similarities. The problem is government. Any government. All government.

Binh Chanh District, Ho Chi Minh City, Viet Nam, May 2000

the phase

Some years ago, during the heady, early days after the lifting of the silly U.S. trade embargo, sitting around the dinner table at Kim Long Quan, Wendell Woon and I were discussing the politics of Viet Nam. Wendell was a fertilizer dealer in Malaysia wanting to develop the Vietnamese market for his products and I had offered to introduce him around to the agriculture community in Ho Chi Minh City and help him make some contacts. We were the original odd couple, the white-boy foreigner driving the brown-boy foreigner around Sai Gon on my Honda with only enough Vietnamese language between us to get us some rice and chicken for lunch. It was wild.

Of course, the politic of Viet Nam is Communism, the very mention of the word striking dread and terror and outrage and despair at the hearts of most Americans. Wendell proposed the notion that "Communism is just a phase that most developing, third world countries go through." My first thought at hearing this was "Sure, great consolation, tell that to all the people who have died at the hands of communist regimes!" In any case I filed this comment for future reference like you'd file a newspaper clipping that you're sure you'd never need again but shouldn't throw away. If he was right I only hoped I would live long enough to see the "phase" pass in this beloved-adopted homeland of mine. I had seen what the system and its abuses had done to the spirit of these people. After 30 years without economic improvement in the North now this political system was driving the South full speed ahead toward destruction like a runaway freight train toward a bridge-out. At least it was, until the Russian "perestroika" and the eventual collapse of this same system in The Soviet Union. This was significant because Viet Nam parallel-adopted "Doi Moi" in '89 as a means of bolstering the mockery of an economy that existed since the April 30, 1975 take over of the South by the Communists. Doi Moi is a relaxing of the strangle hold the communists held on the economy and civil liberties of the country. It was a defacto admission that what existed was failing and something new had to be tried. It worked.

One problem, strange bedfellows were created. Here was a Communist political system that had adopted a Capitalist economic system. The principles and liberties that are necessary for and inherent in Capitalism (land ownership, a free market, individual determination) would certainly have an effect on the totalitarian principals of Communism. And it did. Now, eleven years after Doi Moi, the end of Communism in Viet Nam appears to be inevitable! The sheer weight of a thriving, free market system on the decayed and crippled back of a flawed and corrupt political system foreshadows its collapse. "It ain't broken but it's walkin' with a limp." (T. Waits) Already even the Communists deny that Viet Nam is a Communist country. So many concessions have been made to foreign companies, in order to entice them to come to Viet Nam to do business, that Lenin must surely be rolling in his grave. Roll on Lenin, roll on.

After pondering these change of events in recent years I was taken back to that comment of Wendell Woon's at the dinner table over Hue style escargot. Perhaps he was right and perhaps I will live long enough.

Sai Gon, Viet Nam
May 2000

the hat (for Karla)

It can be deadly...the white light. In your mind, picture the globe that is Daughter-Earth hurling on its annual, appointed track around Mother-Sun. Add to this image the life-giving rays of light striking the surface of the blue planet like buck shot on the belly of an ill-fated Canadian goose. The majority of the buck-shot-rays of light glance off the atmosphere and surface in the Northern and Southern regions but at the Equator, the Tropics, there is no "glancing," only a head-on collision of light and earth...light and animal...light and man. White light.

The Firesign Theater did a skit some years ago entitled "Everything you know is wrong." In 1994 I brought everything I "knew" to this place to apply it to a nursery business that would hopefully benefit many, including me. I soon realized, "Everything I knew was wrong." The first thing I "didn't know" was about the white light. We had to "discover" for ourselves how to handle the extreme intensities in the quality and quantity of sunlight that strikes the Tropical belt of Earth and how to apply this new knowledge to our venture. Some lessons we have to learn the hard way.

The Tropics are notorious for heat. But little is heard of light. The purity and quantity of sunlight here can sear the brain into numbness and cook the skin into cancer. Protection is mandatory! Northerners always wonder at the full covering of the djellaba on the Berber camel herdsmen of the Sahara. Well, these "blue men of the Sahara" know how to protect themselves from the white light and the loose fit of the djellaba provides air flow and a kind of personal "swamp cooler." Here in Viet Nam, most people wear thin, loose, long pants (only foreigners wear shorts) and long-sleeved shirts, a sort of form fitting version of the tent-like djellaba. And everyone wears a hat. The hat is standard issue for all of humanity, from pauper to prince, beggar to banker.

The hat comes in all shapes, sizes, fashion, style, colors, and configurations imaginable. The most common these days is the ubiquitous baseball cap. The baseball cap is the crown on the head of the walking billboard...its wearer. Every company, team, association, or group advertizes their existence on the bill of baseball caps. From Sai Gon Beer to the Chicago Bulls, it's all on the brow of a baseball cap.

The women, as women do, sport much more decorative and stylish headgear. The artistic principle that form follows function is played out to its fullest extent in the myriad of different hats that women wear to protect their heads from the death rays of the white light. As stylish as the hat can be, the "function" aspect is paramount and "form" is secondary.

Of course, the signature hat of the Orient is the conical hat. Most Americans recognize the hat by its less than flattering slang name of "cooly hat" from the Chinese worker-immigrants of the eighteenth century and the stereotypical Hollywood portrayals of all Orientals wearing cooly hats. It's like all Dutch people wear wooden shoes. Come on!

As a hat, the conical reigns supreme. First, in the arena of white light protection it provides a full 360 degree "brim." You'd have to wear four baseball caps at once to provide the same shading as a conical hat. Second, the hat is loose on the head, like the Berber's djellaba is loose on the body. Welcome breezes flow under the hat to cool and refresh the scalp. Third, when the wearer retreats under the shade of a tree or shelter the conical hat can be transformed into a fan to stir stagnant air into a personal breeze by simply holding the edge and waving it at oneself. I've seen it used to fan a smoldering coal back to flame in order to cook Banh Tet and Banh Chung, New Year's rice cakes. The fan usage is probably the second most widely used function for the conical hat after head protection.

The conical hat is by far the most versatile piece of equipment to ever adorn the human body. It's a hat, yes. But it's so much more. Turned upside down it becomes a bowl-like container to transport or collect just about anything. It can be used to carry fruit or flowers or, in the hands of a street beggar, to collect the generous money-gifts of passers by. It's been used to bale a leaking boat or as a portable sink. Find a use for a bowl shaped object and the conical hat has fulfilled it.

The conical hat is functional, durable, cheap and plentiful but more important, it's poetic. The conical hat atop a woman wearing an Au Dai is the purest, physical personification of poetry in the Orient (distantly followed by bamboo and the stork). The Au Dai is the symbol of Vietnamese traditional women's fashion. The outfit consists of loose, long pants and a long "tunic-type" form fitting blouse that almost reaches the ground and is slit up each side to the waist to allow the pants to be seen through the slits. Most times the fabric is one color but often, designs will be created on the chest part of the tunic top and down the front to further enhance the decorativeness of the garment. Place a white conical hat on top of a beautiful, red-lipped Vietnamese woman in an Au Dai and who needs Longfellow or Keats or Confucius.

Brookings, Oregon, January 2001

the hemingway sidebar
(for Orville)

The early days were heady. As with any new
project the "newness" itself makes for excitement
and a thrill of anticipation. I felt like a pioneer in
the old West as one of the first Americans to
come back here after the lifting of the trade
embargo. Sure, there were other foreigners---
Europeans, other Asians, Australians, but few
Americans. I'd go for days and never see
another white boy, especially out in the
agricultural districts where I wandered and
eventually built the nursery. The sheer
excitement of the challenge and the expectations
of success drove me day after day far better than
food or drink. It was as if one could live on work
alone.

On my second trip I partnered up with Mr. Nguyen
Hau. I felt I needed a Vietnamese national to
help with all of the bureaucratic formalities that
became legion in this Socialist corner of Indo-
China after '75. During the building of the nursery
we hired many local workers to help with
construction and planting. We started our days
early before the infamous tropical heat could
establish itself. Of course, the indigenous
peoples of these tropical countries have the good
sense to rest out of the sun and heat of midday.
Only foreigners are crazy enough to continue
through to day's end; hence, the term "mad dogs
and Englishmen" from the English colonial days in
India when the Indian people observed that only

mad dogs and Englishmen were crazy enough to work through the heat of midday. Mad dogs and Englishmen...and Americans!

The construction of the nursery consisted of a bamboo "lath" shade covering over the land and bamboo legged tables with bamboo table tops. As a section of shade cover was completed, another crew would build tables underneath and then the potting crew would cover the tables with the potted plants. The whole nursery grew and "moved" this way from one corner of the land toward the opposite corner like an oil slick from a ruptured super tanker on Prince William Sound.

A group of women workers potted the plants. We ordered a gaggle of pedal powered three wheeled "pick-up trucks" to dump loads of coconut fiber in a mound in the center of our land and the women squatted haphazardly around the pile to pot the seedlings. From afar the scene looked like a surreal reddish Christmas-tree-like mountain decorated with multicolored, pear-shaped ornaments, each capped by white conical peaks. Of course, the pear shapes were the squatted women dressed in their workday worst. One needn't be stylish when doing Ag work. Many just wore old, okay to get grungy, practical work clothes like we'd wear to help our brother-in-law move apartments or fix his dead Toyota. But the common denominator that bound the women together as one was the ubiquitous white conical hat, the stereotypical signature piece of The Orient. The practicality of the conical hat in Asia is a prime illustration of the inscrutable nature of the people themselves. The hat serves as shelter from the sun and doubles as umbrella in the rain and trebles as fan when the need for cooling arises. Often at break the women will fan themselves with their hats as they chatter together, the same chatter that could be heard from any group of women anywhere in the world at break time. The women were potting the 150,000 Tillandsia cyanea I had bought from David Fell in Hawaii and the 9,000 Guzmania seedlings I had imported from Holland. The whole land was abuzz with activity in those early weeks with the sounds of sawing and hammering and instruction calling from crew chiefs to workers. We were the new kids on the flower district block of Go Vap District and we became the talk of the town.

In addition to all of the construction and potting workers, Ong Hau had an inner cadre of staff that would remain after the initial mountain of work was completed to operate the nursery. He had Ong Thi and Ong Viet who would grow the plants and Ong Muoi for a night watchman and guard. Ong Muoi and I hit it off from the beginning. He was in his late 60's and had that warm smile and soft disposition so common amongst elder Vietnamese men. I love the old people here. They've seen it all. The oldest go all the way back before the horrors of the Japanese occupation during World War II and weathered both the French and the American wars and now the Communist regime. Many speak French and English. Ong Muoi had seen it all.

Often I would eat lunch with Ong Muoi. One of the ever present kids of the workers would run down the road to a street vendor and bring back food-to-go for us---sort of Vietnamese McD's.

We'd sit across from each other at the table and nourish ourselves on simple food for simple people. Remember. We're agriculture workers, just simple farmers. Most of the time the food was recognizable---rice, chicken, pork, vegetables, sometimes not. Once there was a small dish of a dark maroon-colored jellied substance surrounded by the other recognizable dishes of foods. It was food to be eaten so I thrust my chop stick into the mass, picked up a glob, and put it in my mouth with a rice chaser. It really didn't taste of anything, just a warm glob of a dark maroon-colored jellied substance. I had no sooner put the substance and rice in my mouth when Ong Muoi and the other workers eating around the table began to giggle like school girls when the cute-boy preppy walks into the cafeteria. I didn't know if I had erred in determining the substance to be food or the substance was food but not for me to eat. Ong Muoi came to my rescue by taking a chop stick full of the substance himself and eating it with a rice chaser mimicking me. He and I and all the workers smiled and then laughed out loud at the episode. I was accepted as one of them on the spot. This white boy is all right. I had just eaten blood.

After eating we'd stretch out on a mat on the ground and stare up at the patterns of the bamboo and palm frond roof over the nursery's shelter. The rhythm of the repeated patterns of bamboo-frond-bamboo-frond would massage the mind and then the body to sleep. I just may have the best life on earth! After an hour or so of rest it was back to work creating the infrastructure that would provide us all with our daily bread.

79

Many times Ong Muoi and I would sit and talk on varied subjects. He had worked for the Americans during the war and was therefore obliged to spend time in the reeducation camps after the April 1975 Communist takeover. During one of our conversations I mentioned I had brought a volume of Hemingway short stories to read in my spare time. When I said the name "Hemingway" his eyes glazed over with a far away look of fantasy and he repeated the name-----"Hemingway." He loved Hemingway. Ong Muoi and I had found a common bond between us that joined us closer yet. Toward the end of my trip I decided to give the volume to him as a gift. I wrote out a note to put in the book and asked Ong Cat, my family's patriarch, to translate it for me and write the translation in the inner cover. The gift readied, I wrapped it and took it to the nursery.

The day I took the gift was to be my last before returning home and after a usual long day's work several of us were sitting out on the sidewalk in front of the nursery. I brought out the package and handed to Ong Muoi. He questioningly looked at me as he took it. Smiling, he opened it, read the cover, opened to the inside cover and read the inscription I had written through Ong Cat. After about a minute of reading he raised his head with eyes filled with tears and got up out of his chair and approached me and surrounded my neck with a big hug. The unusualness of this gesture cannot be over emphasized. Asian people don't hug! Maybe he learned this gesture from the Americans he had worked with. I don't know. But he was so touched and joyful by the gift that this was his reaction. We parted best of friends and remain so to this day though our paths have separated. Two souls brought together for a moment in time to bond and exchange humanity because of a common interest—Hemingway.

Brookings, Oregon
January 2001

the feast

They were charcoal grey and alive and wriggling in the bowl this morning. Tonight they're basketball orange and steaming on the plate covered in a brown, sweet, gingery sauce. I live in a place that catches some of the best crab in the world but no one prepares it like this. Be Chi had pre cracked the hard shells of the man-hand sized crabs and it was a simple matter to snap off a claw and withdraw the tender flesh. After a few bites the sauce covered every finger and most of our chins. As we gathered in a Neanderthal frenzy to feed on the sea bounty a ferocious thunder and lightning storm raged outside. The windows on both ends of the house flashed to white-life with lightning and instantly rattled with deafening thunder as the rain hammered down on the galvanized tin roof like Oklahoma hail. We laughed and talked and ate as if nature's accompaniment was designed for our dinning pleasure.

The crab was followed by a "taco" salad of dried rice noodles, cauliflower, mushrooms, carrots, small bits of beef and covered in a similar sweet sauce as the crab. The hard, wildly curvy dried noodles were a handful with chop sticks and refused to enter the mouth without force. This action added more sauce to our already dripping faces as the noodles snapped around the edges of our mouths. It's funny to me how different peoples can take the very same raw materials and build entirely different end products from them. The storm continued its rant as if carrying on to the next song in the head banger concert.

As the rain washed the midday dust from the roof we washed the feast down with slugs of iced Tiger beer from hard, glass mugs with big handles that could be easily gripped with our slippery and saucy fingers.

Dessert consisted of Jack fruit, the huge, football shaped tropical fruit that grows close to the main trunk of its tree rather than out on the branches like oranges or apples. After breaking open the shell of the fruit the individual seed capsules are extracted and the flesh around the seed is eaten revealing the seed itself which is the size of a golf ball that's been run over by a D-8. Be Chi gave me a Mang Cau or commonly called "grenade". It looks just like a grenade. After peeling off the soft, outer covering the flesh is eaten and the hard, black, pea-sized seeds are spit out like watermelon seeds. Of course the taste is liquid-sugar-sweet.

As we finished the meal the storm subsided as if its sentence had been commuted and it had been released from its obligation. It may be one of the poorest countries in the world but they eat like kings and the entertainment's great. What is poverty?

The Palace, Binh Chanh, Viet Nam
March 17, 2001

deja vu

1971-Franco's Spain

We rode the BMW into Madrid one day along the main road from the North. As we approached the city, we began to notice La Guardia soldiers standing on the overpasses, with their now familiar flat-backed hats and ever-present automatic weapons on their shoulders. Then we noticed them standing on the small hillocks along the road, too. The closer we got to the city, the more Guardia we saw, and the more oppressive the environment became. But then, it was Franco's Spain. We had become used to that. The Guardia were everywhere, Franco's personal police force. Welcome to a police state. (We later discovered that dignitaries were about to use the road for City access and the Guardia were called for security purposes.)

1971-Cold War Berlin

Berlin, the divided city of cold war Europe lies within East Germany. After about a two-hour ride through the countryside of East Germany, over the torturously undulating East German Autobahn, Berlin appears, as if out of a dream from a stark landscape. Crossing the frontier reveals a modern, Western city plunked down in the middle of grayness and deprivation. It's like a blemish of health in the middle of an otherwise cancerous body. After settling into our campsite routine we began to investigate the city. It's divided into four quarters, and each supervised by one of the four victorious ally forces. There are military vehicles everywhere, uniformed personnel everywhere, and a sense of oppression everywhere. At night we hear automatic gunfire. Which side? Did the escapee make it? Or not!

October, 2001-San Francisco International Airport (one month after the September 11th terrorist attacks.)

I set off the metal detector! And this after taking great care to rid myself of all metal objects, to put them in my carry-on or checked bags. I was directed to the man with the wand. He judiciously scanned my body. EVERYTHING set the wand beeping, my watch, my buttons, the little metal decorative chevrons on my shoes, my passport, even my toothbrush. By the time he was finished, everything in my pockets lay in the basket on the counter. He was satisfied. While redressing after the summary strip search I looked up to notice three camouflage-suited army personnel stationed strategically in front of the security inspection station, each with his M-16 lovingly cradled to his breast, reminiscent of a three-decade earlier Spanish incident. There was an air of serious solemnity about the place. If I didn't know better, I'd call it oppression!

The bastards took all the fun out of flying!

Saturday, October 20, 2001, 6:00 A.M.
Seoul, Korea

the game

You know it's coming. The sky has been darkening for over an hour. The thunder rolls in the distance. The gentle, cooling breeze turns to a genuine wind. The breeze caused the shade cloth to gently wave. The wind caused it to whip. As the whipping begins, Thinh and I look at each other from across the nursery and communicate that old married couple's non-verbal communication. "We'd better beef-up the tie downs for the shade cloth so it can withstand the high winds." The wordless communication completed we both return to surveying the coming storm. The sound begins, first a gentle hushing from afar as if in the next room, then, as the rain pelts the banana leaves of the grove beyond the pasture, the hushing turns to a round of applause. When the drops reach the shade cloth they're atomized into a mist over the plants and us. It's time to head for the house. It can be dangerous out here in the nursery during a storm. One time in Go Vap I lingered to enjoy the cooling effect of the rain under the shade cloth and a bolt of lightening exploded right above my head. The steel pillars of the shade structure make perfect lightening rods.

We all made a "FloJo" dash for the shelter of the house from the nursery area. As the rain slammed into the tin roof the applause turned to a standing ovation. We closed the windows on the windward side to stop the horizontal rain and opened them on the lee. We were safe and now there was nothing to do but wait. Anh Dai pulled out a primitive, hand-made Chinese Chess game from under the wooden bed structure in the kitchen and he and Anh Ti sat cross legged across from each other with the board wedged in between. They arranged the pieces and began the game. I've seen this game played many times on the city streets by the old men and the vigor with which the pieces are slammed down on the board to denote the taking of the opponents piece is always humorous. The conquer instinct never dies. As the two boys played, Co Xa found a magazine to read and curled up on the floor next to the boys and I found a chair to oversee the whole operation while Thinh lit a few blessing incense to place around the house. The boys played along for awhile with the strategy, sacrifice, and kill of the chess game and then Thinh came up to advocate for Ti, the younger and less experienced. Thinh suggested the next move and sometimes in frustration just reached down and made the move. The three laughed and talked non stop as the game progressed. When there was a lag time for thinking Thinh turned to me and said, "When I was in the re-education camp we played this game day and night. The communists made us go to bed at nine o'clock every night and would not permit us to play any later so we would cover the board and ourselves with a blanket and play by candle light." The more experienced Dai was victorious over the younger boy. The game wound down with the subsiding storm as if pre-planned. Ti slipped the board and pieces back under the table and we all headed back out to the nursery. Dai had conquered Ti. The storm had conquered Cu Chi.

We went home to a dinner party with Dinh and Toa beginning with a pea/potato salad formed in the shape of a fish on a fish shaped plate with a real fish head at one end of the formed salad to complete the illusion of a fish. Sliced carrots were arranged on the formed salad to simulate fish scales. This first course was followed by Hue-style escargot. (These are the baseball size snails which are so famous in Viet Nam.) The meal finished up with a noodle, liver, shrimp, vegetable and mushroom soup with watermelon dessert and the ubiquitous iced Sai Gon beer. It's tough duty here but someone has to do it.

Binh Chanh, Viet Nam
October 25, 2001

the rats

It was English time in Miss Purdle's second grade class. The lesson plan called for the teacher to ask the students to give a word for each letter of the alphabet as she asked. Miss Purdle dreaded this task because of Ronnie. Ronnie was an active, likable kid with a shock of blond hair that always had a cowlick on the top in back that stood straight up. The problem was, he always came up with profane, cuss words as examples for the letters of the alphabet. Miss Purdle could always expect a ripe four letter word from Ronnie on this assignment. "Who has a word for the letter A?" Ronnie's hand shot up waving in excitement with a ready answer. Miss Purdle ignored him and called on Mary. "Apple." "Very good Mary. B?" Ronnie's hand shot up again undaunted. "Darrel?" "Baseball." "Thank you Darrel. C?" Miss Purdle continued through the alphabet while also continuing to ignore the perseverant Ronnie and his waving hand. Finally she got to the letter R. She thought to herself that R must be a "safe" letter to call on Ronnie to answer. He surely can't think of a cuss word that starts with the letter R. "R?" "Okay, Ronnie. What's your word?" "RATS" he said with a satisfied grin and then held up both hands to indicate size and said "BIG FUCKIN' RATS." "Oh Ronnie." Miss Purdle exclaimed in exasperation.

It was about four in the morning and I heard a sound downstairs, or was it in the street or next door. I ignored it. Another sound came from the same direction. It couldn't be a robber, this house is perfectly secure and a robber wouldn't be that clumsy twice. Then a large CRASH came from the kitchen. I pulled the mosquito net up and slipped out of bed heading for the kitchen. I met Thinh in the hallway. "What was that?" "I don't know." He said. We turned on the light and proceeded down the stairs with caution. Halfway down I could see the entire kitchen and livingroom and could verify that it wasn't a robber. I walked over to the gate-door that leads out to the wash area behind the kitchen and there was a broken washtub on the floor. I looked to the right and saw a rat on top of the wash rack. "It's a rat!" I screamed with excitement. Thinh unlocked the gate, picked up a handy stick and headed in the rat's direction. The rat ran into the kitchen right past me and then down the short staircase to the living room and over to the far corner. After screeching like a girl in a comic strip I followed the rat to the corner and yelled "There he is!" Thinh came over and proceeded to wack aimlessly at the vermin. It ran back to the kitchen and wash room with me following and yelling "There it is!" and Thinh following and wacking aimlessly. This Keystone comedy went on for about a half hour back and forth "There he is!" Wack, wack. "There he is!" Wack, wack. Back and forth. Finally one time in the livingroom Thinh connected. The dazed creature lay there wriggling long enough for Thinh to wack him again. "He's still moving! Hit him again!" He did and it was over. The two great white hunters (well one was brown) bagged their game. We stood triumphantly over the defeated creature and pondered where we should hang its trophy head on the wall. It was a big fuckin' rat.

I've never seen so many rats as I saw last night coming home from the airport. I must have seen half a dozen run across the road as we drove. Thinh says because of the rain they can't live in their holes in the ground so they're out in public more. We went back to bed but sleep was useless after our adventure. We arose at six and Be fixed us Pho and café sua da, my favorite iced coffee. After a leisurely morning we went to the nursery. It's MORE beautiful than the photos! Everything is clean and well organized and the plants have had several months to clean themselves up after the trauma of the move. We unpacked the boxes of seedlings I brought and then sat down to a duck and cucumber lunch that Be had sent with us. We washed it down with iced Sai Gon beer. Ain't life grand! (By the way, Ba Nga met me at the airport last night and whisked me through customs and agriculture inspection as usual. Bless her heart!)

After our post lunch nap on the cool floor of our house we began to pot the seedlings until about 4:00 and headed home. We had not gone far when we came upon an accident. Several motorcycles in a pile and many bodies and lots of blood. Maybe death. We drove home in a somber mood as it began to rain.

It's a rough place.

Sunday evening, October 21, 2001
Cu Chi, Viet Nam

the ant and the cicada

The 17th century French poet and fabulist, Jean de La Fontaine, has a fable about the ant and the cicada. The ant works all summer long going forth and back collecting food for the winter. Always working, forth and back, collecting, working. The cicada spends the summer in the trees singing. Singing, singing all day long while the ant works below. When winter arrives the cicada becomes hungry and goes to the ant to ask for food. The ant asks the cicada "What did you do all summer?" The cicada replies "I was singing!" "Then sing again. I have no food for you." the ant responded.

I first met the cicada in Singapore in '95 when I was looking for export customers for our plants. (Timothy Mc Vey had just shocked the world with his dastardly deed in Oklahoma.) I walked over to the famous Singapore Botanical Garden from the hotel and was greeted by the screaming sound of their song like the siren luring Odysseus and his men to their deaths. The sound was deafening and inescapable and its origin undefinable. "It must be coming from the trees" I only imagined to myself and later learned about the animal. The Vietnamese children love the sound of the cicada because it foretells the coming of summer and their three month vacation from school.

We have cicada in Cu Chi. As we left the nursery today the now familiar scream of the summer insect began to engulf our senses as we approached the tree where they were perched.

When we reached the tree there was only sound...no thinking, no acting, no escaping...only sound. Thinh and I looked knowingly at each other and smiled and after passing the tree at some distance he broke into one of his soft spoken Vietnamese lessons for me by relating the La Fontaine story. He reminisced about his childhood, catching the insect in a jar and watching the vibrating motion of the inner "wings" as the animal "sang" its song. For a moment Thinh was eight again.

My Father taught me how to work like an ant and for that I'm grateful but sometimes I long for the life of the cicada.

Cu Chi, Ho Chi Minh City
Viet Nam
April 25, 2002

the traffic

The traffic's worse. Coming back from the nursery, chugging through the soup of unburned gasoline fumes and the smoke of burned diesel fuel and the honking at all decibel levels and the people talking and the motorcycles and cars and trucks and buses growling at each other and the general din of evening rush hour traffic in the city, Thinh plugs in a tape. Jim Morrison wales:

Love me two times girl
I'm goin' away
Love me two times
Once for tomorrow
Once just for today
Love me two times
I'm goin' away

Sounds good to me but who needs an excuse? Life is full of juxtapositions if you just look around a little.

Everything still looks good. Thinh and Be still look good. The "Palace" still looks good. The nursery still looks good. The city bustles more but otherwise still looks good. Arriving last night, Ba Nha met me as I entered the immigration area and motioned me toward the diplomat desk. "Chao Ba Nha." "Chao Ong Ron" she replied. "Chao Co" I addressed the stern-faced immigration official (Immigration officials all over the world are stern-faced.). "Chao Ong" she replied as her face cracked into a suggestion of a smile, only a suggestion. She entered my name in her computer and did her official duties which culminated with the thump, thump, thump of the stamping in my passport and entry documents and I was on my way feeling like a "diplomat who carried on his shoulders a siamese cat" (Dylan). "Cam on Co." I thanked her and went with Ba Nha to retrieve my boxes of plants.

After about the third air container, there they were, and I muscled them onto my cart and headed for customs hot on the heels of Ba Nha. She motioned me to put the boxes on the x-ray belt while she worked her magic with the customs official. I re-muscled my boxes back onto the cart after x-ray and jumped on her heels again heading for the exit door. Thinh hailed me from across the fence and we met at the exit gate. I gave Ba Nha her "thank you gift," loaded the boxes in the car, and we headed for the Palace. The whole entry procedure took maybe ten minutes. Friendship in high places is wonderful!

Your rulers are rebels,
And companions of thieves;
Everyone loves a bribe,
And chases after rewards.
Isaiah 1:23

Land prices in Cu Chi are skyrocketing. In just one year our land has increased in value ten times. Not bad for a year's work. The bad part is we can't afford to buy any more. Some day we'll build a villa on the land and sell it for a million. No joke.

It's hotter in Cu Chi than in Sai Gon but it's peaceful and the city-traffic sounds of motorcycles and cars and trucks and buses are replaced with the country-traffic sounds of motorcycles and cows and birds and dogs. (Of course the motorcycles are like God...they're omnipresent.) I remember in '94 when Go Vap was in the country, too. I sat in front of the nursery to watch the coming storms accompanied by the same country sounds of motorcycles and cows and birds and dogs. How long will it take the city to reach Cu Chi? Many of the displaced flower farmers from Go Vap District have moved to Cu Chi and a new "Flower District" is emerging. We have fallen into the classic "being in the right place at the right time!" We finally did something right! The plants are growing much better in Cu Chi also, partially due to better water quality. The leaves are dark green and shiny with no tip burn. The flowers have better color also. The water IS better but most of this improved plant quality is due to Thinh's gain in experience and knowledge. He's gone from a professional accountant to a professional horticulturist in six years. Remarkable.

A soulful, Vietnamese torch song is playing on the TV now while the crackling sounds of deep-frying shrimp come from the kitchen as Be prepares dinner. A welcome cloud cover came in this afternoon to subdue the oppressive April heat but it's dark now so it's quite comfortable in the prop-wash of the humming fan behind me. I just spread on my mosquito repellant to ward off the little buggers. There are two sizes of mosquitoes here. The small ones fly right through the weave of the mosquito netting, the big ones just lift it up and come right in. I think my body finally reached the International Date Line between Alaska and

Russia. After another night's sleep it'll arrive in Viet Nam to meet me. Just a little lag. I think I'll let it catch up now.

Sai Gon, Viet Nam
April 21, 2002

bumpty-bump-bump

It's Friday night in Sai Gon...Bumpty-Bump-Bump. Trouble is it's not Sai Gon-by-night. It's just not the same in a taxi. It could be Kansas City-by-night, London-by-night, New Delhi-by-night...all cities are the same from inside the sterile bubble of a taxi cab. No, Sai Gon-by-night can only be experienced on a motorcycle. You have to rub elbows with the family of four on a Honda and the cigarette smoking, speeding bad boys and the hot little numbers in the short, skimpy halter tops with the long pointy shoes. Now that's Sai Gon-by-night!

We just left a restaurant at the corner of Minh Khai Street and Cach Mang Thang 8 Street (The August Revolution Street). How many of those little two-wheeled one lungers must have passed that intersection in the hour we were eating? Say at least 50 (more?) per green light...50...50...50...we were there for over an hour. I'll bet 10,000 motorcycles passed us in that hour. Sai Gon-by-night! And dinner...shrimp boiled in sweet oil, a baby squid and vegetable platter, fish soup with pineapple, chicken cooked from the inside from a burning shaft of bamboo with sweet, green sticky rice, and the piece-de-resistance...frog...no, not just the legs, the whole frog splayed out on the plate like a high school science project ready for dissection and devouring by the epicurean scholastic. "Here, try one more dish. You won't die!"

We had come back from the Mekong Delta today. In the over 30 trips to this place I really haven't had much opportunity to see the sights. It's always been arrive-work-depart...arrive-work-depart...over 30 times in ten years. Pamela's seen more of the country than I have. Fortunately, thanks to Be Chi, Thinh's wife, with her good ideas, the last few times I've been able to play tourist a little. Last time we took a two day trip to Da Lat and now this day trip to the Delta to see the My Thuan bridge over the Mekong River. The bridge was just completed recently and we all have been anxious to see it. It was built with help from the Australians and is a modified suspension bridge. From afar it looks very spider webby, juxtaposed like an apostrophe on the text of the banana/palm tree/rice field landscape of the Delta. It adds a Sci-fi, other-worldly aspect to this timeless agrarian setting.

Thinh's sister, Co Phoung, and her daughter, Co Hanh, joined Be Chi, Thinh, and me this morning at the tourist office downtown after a rushed taxi ride through the morning commuter traffic. We were afraid we would miss the bus so we dropped Thinh off to take a Honda Om through the traffic to hold the bus for our arrival. Just as we arrived the bus was ready to leave. Perfect timing! We traveled for three hours through the heart of the most productive rice growing area on planet earth, each paddy neatly laid out with the tomb of the ancestors right in the middle and their spirits watching over the farm. The greens don't exist on an artist's palate...only in the rice paddies of the Mekong Delta.

Upon our arrival at the river we took a small tourist boat out to Cai Be, the floating market. Here many of the people live on their boats and ply their wares from boat to boat. Each vendor's product is displayed atop a tall bamboo pole for identification. If a vendor is selling watermelons then a watermelon is stuck on top of the bamboo. Most of the boats are driven by what looks like single cylinder Briggs and Stratton engines turning a long shaft with a propeller on the end. The motor/shaft/propeller assembly pivots on the transom of the rudderless boat for guidance by the driver, pivoting the whole assembly left and right. The river is alive with the blat, blat, blat of the single cylinders toiling their way through the café-au-latte water of the Mekong as it relentlessly surges toward the South China Sea and Cambodia.

After an hour or so boating around the market we crossed the main river and went up a small canal to dock for rice/pork chop/vegetable lunch and viewing of the making of rice candies and a serenade by local farmer/musicians. There was a woman singer and two stringed instrument players. One of the instruments was a modified Spanish guitar with the high E string removed leaving only five strings and the wood between the frets concavely carved out to leave a deep space for the player to press and stretch the strings to obtain the ubiquitous vibrato of oriental music. The other instrument was a two stringed "banjo" looking device with high frets off the neck for the same purpose as the guitar, to vibrato the note. I think Alanis Morrisette took singing lessons from this woman. She did vibrato things in the back of her throat, without moving her lips, that sounded surreal and sensually animal-like. Oh yea, the guitar player had a foot operated percussion device to keep the beat that had the hollow knock-knock-knock sound of the young boy's in the streets of Sai Gon tapping out their rhythms with a stick on the half bamboo. The whole thing was very cliched-Oriental…very mellow…very sweet.

After docking we walked through the market of Vinh Long with all the fruits and vegetables and house wares of everyday living. If it wasn't there…well…you didn't really need it anyway. The fruit displays are particularly beautiful not only because of the bright colors but also because of the arrangement of the display with the fruits neatly stacked in pyramids. The produce managers at Raley's could learn something here!

On the bus ride back we stopped for a short rest in My Tho at a bonsai garden with caged monkeys and boas for accent. The final hour of bus ride returned us to the tourist office in Sai Gon and then the short walk to the restaurant. It was a good day. Be Chi has good ideas.

Sai Gon---Thanh Pho Ho Chi Minh
Viet Nam
September 24, 2004

Tuesday is "Children's Day" mid-Autumn Festival. Every corner has stands selling moon cake.

the allure

We left Ong Cat's house tonight for dinner down on Nam Ky Khoi Nghia Street downtown. Over the smelly canal, past the Pagoda and its cloud of sweet but overpowering incense (today is Buddha's birthday) and into the beating heart of the city we rode. Every Honda ever produced is rolling tonight...Sunday night...gotta get out ...cut loose...show off...see who's out...be seen...make the scene.

Dinner began with small conical snails in a sweet brown sauce. The small end of the cone-shell had been broken off so you could hold your finger tip over the hole and then suck on the big end to build up a good vacuum and then release your finger to propel the animal out of its shell and into your mouth like a snotty bullet. Life doesn't get any better! Vegetables with small rice cakes followed and finally a soup tureen over a burner on the table to cook our own fish, shrimp, squid, octopus, and vegetables completed the feast. Of course this was all whetted down with Tiger beer and unknown pink and green drinks. They had to roll us out with hand trucks.

All around, the restaurant buzzed with the excitement of release and enjoyment...families, couples, groups of boys, groups of girls, groups of boys and girls, foreigners...all laughing and talking loud and eating and drinking and more laughing and talking loud. The place throbbed with noise. The waitresses shouted orders to the cooks over tables from across the room. Bus boys and bus girls clanged dishes and silverware and bottles from the previous diners to make way for the next gang. The fans whirred their refreshing breath over the revelers. It's constant movement, sound and chaos all stirred together with good food. Everyone has their cell phone. I think Darwin was right...we just evolved again...now we have five fingers on one hand and five fingers and a cell phone on the other. It's a rite of passage, it's a symbol, it legitimizes...it's a curse.

After dinner we took a short Sai-Gon-By-Night ride around the park behind the Cathedral and the Post Office where the lovers lined up, sitting on their motorcycles, two by two, locked in heated animal-embrace or silent conversation and broke out into the flood of light and sound that is Nguyen Hue Street. The allure of the city is magnetic and primal and temptuous. It draws without mercy like the deadly flame draws the innocent moth. It could be L.A., San Francisco, New York, London, Paris...tonight it's Sai Gon...tomorrow night it'll be Rio, Lagos, Madras, Hong Kong. How ya gonna keep 'em down on the farm? Ya ain't! Let's face it Toto, this ain't Kansas an' we're not goin' back. Send me my inheritance Dad...I'll see ya when it runs out...maybe.

May 22, 2005
Sai Gon, Viet Nam

the shower

When I'm home, people ask me "Ron, what do you like to do in Viet Nam?" I fire back immediately, "Take a shower!" It's true, I live for the shower. I shower when I wake in the morning, shower at noon before lunch, shower in the afternoon before dinner, shower at night before bed. I'm so clean, when I walk down the street, I squeak! ... rreeek... rreeek... rreeek... rreeek! Why so many showers? It's hot! It's that relentless tropical sun with its malignant rays of white light, white heat. It's more than hot, it's humid. My folks were stationed in Florida during World War II and when I was a kid my Mother would tell me about the humidity in Florida and how it made you sticky and wet all the time and after a shower you never really dried off. Growing up in California I never really understood what she meant. After my first visit to Viet Nam I understood completely.

I first learned of taking multiple showers a day from Be Chi. When I first came here Be and Thinh lived in her Mother's house. I noticed that Be's hair always seemed a little wet and she wore different outfits all day long. Finally I asked why she changed her clothes so often each day and she told me she took many showers each day to cool off. The light went on in my head. I asked her if I could do the same and she agreed. I've been doing it ever since. The bathroom in Be's Mother's house that we used didn't really have running water. There was a faucet that filled a large, plastic container in the room. When you wanted water you used a sauce-pan size "ladle" to scoop water from the big container and then pour the water into the sink or into the toilet to flush or over your body for a shower. I cherished the pouring of the water over my body for its refreshing coolness after a long work day at the nursery. It was heaven in the bathroom. The ritual of the showers continued after Be and Thinh moved to their own house (The Palace) several years later with the addition of running water in the bathroom and to the shower. Gone were the large container and the ladle and in their place was the common shower head to dispense the cooling shower water. It was still heaven...just another bathroom.

Now there are other things I like to do in Viet Nam. One of the best things is riding the Hon Da around the city. Riding the motorcycle gets me right up close to the people in the rolling flow of humanity on bicycles, motorcycles, three-wheelers, cars, buses, and trucks in the elbow to elbow and exhaust pipe to front tire traffic. The traffic is the Great Equalizer. It's like the butch haircut in basic training for the military. Everyone becomes equal when they're stuck in traffic on the motorcycle. My most memorable time of motorcycle riding was during the heady early days of our business at the Tet holiday. We had two market locations in the city to sell our plants the week before Tet. At this time our nursery was still in Go Vap District, behind the airport, and we could easily re-stock our market stalls by motorcycle each day. This became my main duty that week. We would begin the day at 3:00 or 4:00 in the morning and ride to the nursery before the city woke. I had a box behind me on the seat full of plants, another in front of me between my knees and resting on the gas tank and a plastic bag hanging from the end of each handle bar, all filled with plants and tied on with bungee cords. I looked like a flower "Grapes of Wrath" heading for the "Promised Land". I could do two trips in the morning, two trips in the afternoon and one more in the evening when Thinh and I would go collect the money from the day's sales and return home about 11:00 PM. Forth and back...forth and back. It was exhausting work that ended each day with a satisfied collapse in bed and a pocket full of money. (After Tet we all collapsed and slept for three days straight!) By the way, each time I returned to the nursery to re-fill my motorcycle transport I'd take a "shower" by simply ladling water over my head, clothes and all, from the ceramic water container. It was still heaven...who needs a bathroom?

(I'm going to take a break now. Thinh just said we are going somewhere right now for "entertainment". I'll continue when we return.)

...We just returned. Be's brother, Hung, took us to a swimming pool resort just outside the city for the afternoon. His two girls came with us and he left them with us while he went off to get drunk with his friends. When we were ready to go home he was too drunk to drive so he gave the car to Thinh to drive us home while he went back to his friends. I just want to slap that boy some times. On the way back the sky fell just like Chicken Little said it would with drops the size of goose eggs. Even the city gets a shower. (It's funny, with the very first drop, instantly all of the bicyclists and motorcyclists are wearing slickers. They can put them on so fast you don't even notice it.)

Okay, maybe these stories about the showers and the motorcycle rides are entertaining and informative and maybe even a little amusing, and even though they're true, my favorite activity in Viet Nam is just BEING with the people. After we leave all of our meaningless political, economic, racial, and social differences on the shore and wade out into that boundless sea of humanity together, naked, we're all pretty much the same. We all have the same needs and desires and hopes for ourselves and our families and our small differences fade into the horizon.

I'm feeling hot and sticky. I think I'm going to take a shower now.

The Palace, Binh Tan District, Ho Chi Minh City, Viet Nam
May 25, 2005

the theory

I've been working on a theory. It began in a vaporous state many years ago, progressing to liquefaction over the past couple of years and has finally congealed into solidification this week, at least enough to put to paper. For those of you who know me and have followed the saga of my "Viet Nam Project" over the years through these stories, I hope that you will regard me as the eternal optimist. Please flatter me by saying "Yes". Where there is darkness I'm the one who seeks out, finds, and embraces that small ray of light. Here is my latest discovery of small rays of light:

In observing the remarkable events after Perestroika in the Soviet Union and Doi Moi in Viet Nam where the iron fist of Communism was relaxed a little to allow the introduction of the economic system of Capitalism, I can't help but wonder what phenomena lie ahead with similar reforms occurring in China. The seeming diametrical opposites of the totalitarianism of the Communist political system and the boundless liberties of the Capitalist economic system make for the strangest of bedfellows. The result that I have observed in Viet Nam has been the releasing of the jackboot-on-the-neck of more than ten years of Communist rule after 1975 to a situation of freedom and liberty (albeit mostly in the realm of business) that was unheard of just ten years ago. Viet Nam is a Communist country in name only now. To further clarify this statement, I don't mean "Communist in name only" by the current American understanding of

Communism. In Asia the word "Communist" has softened with time as the old hard liners have died out and younger, more forward thinking politicians have taken charge. It's a changing world and Communism has changed with it. The economic failures of the five and ten year plans and the failed nationalized industries have become painfully apparent to the new political leaders and they have looked to Capitalism for their salvation. (Follow the money?)

China has also done this. The Chinese Communists have embarked on a possibly dangerous journey that may threaten their own political existence…they have introduced Capitalism. They have opened a bottle, to release something that can only be recaptured with bloodshed. The danger lies in the fact that embodied in the principals of Capitalism are the essentials of freedom…self-determination rather than the group-determination of the Communist doctrine. (Interestingly this "self determination" of Capitalism and Western thought has risen out of the Judeo/Christian/Greco/Roman/English Common Law heritage that we Westerners share which elevates individualism as opposed to the Confucian philosophy which anchors Eastern thought and its elevation of the group over the individual.)

The problem lies in the fact that when a person is allowed to bite from the enchilada of freedom, the insatiable desire for the whole enchilada arises! When people taste something good they want more. What if the Chinese people, having taken that first bite, want it all? Now this may not mean a complete overthrow of the political system but it may mean a neutering of the system…rendering it impotent. This is what I have seen in Viet Nam. Complete democratization of China may be too big a step right now and may be unnecessary. A neutralized Communist system may be an acceptable first step that we can live with now and save the next step for future generations. What does an impotent Chinese political system mean for despotic regimes like North Korea and radical Middle Eastern Islamic nations? It makes my mind swim to think of the possibilities!

Uncle Ho and Chairman Mao are dead and gone. Could the political systems they installed be far behind?

Ho Chi Minh City
Viet Nam, May 2005

the prodigal

After breakfast and e-mail updates Thinh and I headed for the nursery. The Trans-Asia highway is finally complete to Cam Pu Chia and ultimately Thailand. Thinh says there's a bus service now all the way. In any case, it's good to have the construction done and an easy and safe drive to work.

Co Xa, Anh Dai, and Anh Hai are on duty and greet me with big smiles, firm hand shakes, and "Chao Ong Ron". After some light conversation Co Xa invites Thinh and me to lunch over at Dai's house. She says she'll call her husband to kill the fatted rabbit for a luncheon feast to celebrate the return of The Prodigal from squandering his youth on cheap women, expensive whisky and loud rock 'n roll. Now, I know what you're thinking. "Oh, Ron, not another story about food." But wait, how many stories of Jesus centered on the institution of eating, from the disciples harvesting wheat as they passed through the field to dinner at Mary and Martha's to the feeding of the 5,000? Hey, I'm in divine company!

Co Xa runs off to call her husband. She's a round-faced beauty with a ready smile and big, brown sparkling eyes and has been with us from the beginning 12 years ago. We've grown up together. She was one of the women we first hired to pot the 9,000 Dutch seedlings and the 150,000 cyanea seedlings back in '94. She's still here, faithful and reliable and moved with us to Cu Chi from Go Vap in 2001. Last summer a dog ran out in front of her Honda and she fell and broke her leg putting her out of commission for a while. She's okay now and back to work.

Xa's son is Hai. He's just a kid starting out in the work world and may have an overdose of piss and vinegar. He's been experimenting with stealing and irresponsible youthful behavior and maybe drugs. Before I leave this time I'm going to take him aside and give him a verbal ass kicking. He may listen to me. Or maybe he won't.

Dai is the backbone of the nursery. He has proven himself to be trustworthy and reliable and a hard worker. He married about two years ago and lives right behind the nursery on his grandmother's land. In addition to his day labors he's our night guard, sleeping in the nursery house. On top of all of his good work skills he can cook, hence, the delegation of cooking duties to him for the luncheon feast.

While the three of them headed off to prepare lunch, Thinh and I discussed nursery matters in the cool of the house in front of the fan. Over the years we've had so many communication blockades and break-throughs you'd think we each spoke a different language. Wait a minute. We do speak a different language. Maybe that's been the problem. Today was no exception. After about an hour of discussion we realized we had been misunderstanding each other on one important subject for several years. This was one of those blessed break-through moments! We came out the other side with a common understanding and a new direction for one aspect of the business. Hooray!

Xa called us to lunch and Thinh and I walked to
Dai's house under the steamy noon sun. Dai
lives in one unit of a three-apartment house. His
Father lives with the youngest of his four wives
next door and another tenant next to him. As we
entered, Dai and Xa were still in the kitchen
cooking, Dai boiling the rabbit in coconut milk and
spices and Xa preparing the salad on the floor
next to him. I went out front to sit on the porch to
rest my aching knee and Thinh joined me for a
short wait. Hai was just returning with an armload
of ice and Sai Gon Beer. Moments later we were
called to the front room. Now, remember your
grandmother who kept her house so clean you
could eat off the floor? That was Dai's front
room. The floor had been set with two big bowls
of coconut rabbit and bowls of lettuce and
cucumber and tomato and a bowl of French
bread and eating bowls and spoons and chop
sticks and beer mugs. The feast was ready. We
sat cross legged, filled our bowls with food and
glasses with beer and toasted and ate and drank
with gusto and laughter and camaraderie. Life is
good! We had just started to eat when a man
unknown to me came in and was invited to join us
for lunch. Thinh introduced Thanh to me as the
man we had bought our land from in 2001. They
all bantered in Vietnamese and left me to my own
thoughts and eating. After some time Thanh
remarked that he was amazed that I would eat
their food. He said foreigners and even Viet Kieu
would not eat their food for fear of getting sick. I
told him if he could eat it, then I could too. He
nodded approval. I got another nod from Dai as I
discovered the liver parts of the rabbit. When Dai
realized I liked the liver he dug through the pile of

parts to pull out all of the liver for me and they all laughed with approval.

The food was endless and the beer mugs were constantly topped off until full capacity was reached by all. Everyone agreed Dai had succeeded in satisfying the huddled masses and was elevated to most high status. Thanks Anh Dai!

Thinh and I walked back to the nursery under a clear blue cap of sky with voluminous cumulus clouds crowding the margins, waiting, with their life giving moisture, to be beckoned to work by the Mekong winds. Thinh parked me in a hammock under the shade of a bamboo grove behind the gate to the nursery and I felt like one of the truck drivers waiting outside the city for the rush hour to end so they could deliver their goods. The drivers sling hammocks under the belly of their trucks and wait out the traffic. Well, why not, after all, I'm a truck driver.

After a short nap we locked up the nursery and headed home by side streets to the main road past the Beer Om with the prostitutes and hustlers and heroin dealers loitering out front. There's something for everyone here.

Cu Chi, Viet Nam
October 23, 2006

the diversion--It's not all work

Mornings in the city are the best. The air is clean and cool and the pall of dust and gasoline fumes and diesel smoke hasn't yet fallen on the urban plane. The sleepy-eyed street vendors with their push carts are beginning to line the streets to nourish another day's clientele with the simple breakfast's of the masses. Men sit at the sidewalk tables of the cafes reading the morning paper and drinking their tea or Café Sua and arguing the socio-political events of the day. The school children dutifully parade to their "jobs" to learn the skills that will provide for the next generation of workers and entrepreneurs and officials. They all wear their distinct uniforms that represent their own school and the high school girls in their white Au Dai's ride their bicycles with the tails of the blouses flowing gracefully in the breeze, looking like misty apparitions in a dream scape. It's light but no sunshine yet. The relentless heat is hours away.

We arrived at the tourist office early enough to catch our own morning Café Sua at the adjoining café. Thinh ordered croissants to fill the belly's empty hole after the night-sleep. The street is teeming with tourists and the associated trade that caters to them...the street sellers, the beggars, the thieves and hustlers. "Gotta watch what you're doin'." (Larry Norman) We're headed for the beach resort of Mui Ne in Phan Thiet Province. This is the home of nuoc mam, the fish sauce juice that defines Vietnamese cuisine. There are also many groves of Thanh Long or Dragon Fruit, the fuchsia colored fruit of the epiphyllum plant. This is one of my favorite fruits here. The flesh is snow white and dotted with tiny black seeds and when cut open the fuchsia colored skin surrounds the white and black interior like a framed masterpiece. The sweetness is just subtle enough to tease the palate for more and the seeds add a texture of graininess similar to Kiwi.

Man's cruelty to man: We read in the paper on the bus trip about a couple who had been arrested for going into the countryside and taking young boys from their families and conscripting them to beg on the streets of Ho Chi Minh City. Of course, the boys were required to bring all of the proceeds of their efforts back to the couple and if their take was insufficient they were beaten or deprived of food. I hope the couple's next address is an equally cruel establishment of punishment for a very long time.

We're going to Da Lat later so we're required to spend another day here in order to catch the morning bus. To pass the day we took a minivan trip with other tourists to "surf" the white sand dunes near by. Along the road we passed fishing villages and coves scattered with blue-cabined fishing boats as if Neptune himself had rolled a handful of boats like dice on an emerald table and they moored where they fell. Our driver turned down a trail off the main road and headed for the rolling hills beyond. A lake emerged on our left with lotus pads growing on the margins. The white pods and the pink flowers dotted the green pads over the brown water with white-white sand dunes on the far shoreline all framed by a crystal blue sky. We arrived at the entrance to the dunes to be greeted by young boys who would escort us to the dunes for the surfing experience. One youngster, Hanh, latched on to me and appointed himself personal guide for the time. He was thirteen and could easily have passed for eight. He led me ahead of the others and the two of us struck out for the dunes. Along the way he took my hand and compared his own to the size of mine. The two of our hands together looked like the beast King Kong holding the tiny and frail hand of Fay Rey. Along the way he stopped at a café to pick-up a plastic sheet about man-size (Vietnamese man not King Kong-man) and we continued to walk toward the dunes looming in the distance. We climbed to the top of a near dune and found the lee side to plunge steeply into the next valley. Ah, just like Tahoe but not freezing cold! He laid the plastic down on the ground, ordered me to lie face down on it and pull the front edge up like the leading edge of a toboggan, then, from behind, he raised my feet so my legs were bent at the knees and began to push King Kong-on-plastic-sheet over the side into the "valley of death". I didn't quite get up to toboggan speed but it was fast enough to illicit uncontrollable laughter. That was fun! Let's do it again! Oh, oh! Wasn't it Einstein or Newton or Wilbur Wright or maybe it was Alfred E. Newman who said "What goes down must come back up again." Trudge. Trudge. Trudge. Maybe just one more time after my heart recovers from arrest. This time I sat cross legged on the plastic and ordered Hanh to get on behind me. He pushed like the last rider on the Luge run at the winter Olympics and jumped on. We had not gone far when the whole of our mechanism…King Kong, Fay Rey, and plastic sled…began to yaw sideways until, perpendicular to the slope, we overturned and proceeded the rest of the way down the hill ass over tea kettle, laughing hysterically all the way. We rolled to a stop at the bottom like two rejected rag dolls with sand covering our sweated bodies like a couple of breaded fish ready to be fried. What fun!

We left Mui Ne in a twelve passenger minivan heading north for the main road where we will catch a bigger bus for Da Lat. The air conditioner mocked us with inefficiency so we gave it the boot and opened the windows. The outside humidity was more comforting than the inside stupefaction. We generally followed the coast but only rarely saw the water and the fishing villages and boats. Most of the trip was inland a little through sparsely populated countryside. As we raced along in our rolling missile it occurred to me that once leaving the socio/economic/political centers of a civilization and traveling through the countryside the sameness of life's existence emerges. We could be in the countryside of Kansas or Iowa. The café signboard that reads Com Ga-3,000 Dong could read Ham' an Eggs-3 Bucks. The Honda parked out front could be a Ford pick-up. The rice field behind the café could be wheat. And the man sitting at the table in the café could be wearing a baseball cap with a Cubs logo on the brow rather than the bamboo conical hat of a Vietnamese farmer. Sameness abounds minimizing differences. And the life-blood of the men is identical. The wheels and pulleys and gears and bearings of the mechanism that make up the biology of the men and the lubricating life-blood of these mechanisms are identical. The skin may be a different color and the tongue may form different sounds behind the lips but the whole of the mechanism is the same.

We passed through a small village with horn honking announcement of our arrival to disperse wayward pedestrians. One young man looked up at our van and saw me looking at him. His mouth broadened into a white, toothy smile and his hand shot up in a wave as I mirrored his actions. For that instant in time we were brothers, fellow life travelers, like two atoms smashed together in an accelerator and suddenly ripped apart again by the progress of our rolling missile.

Once reaching the main road we transferred to the bigger bus for the final trip into the pine forested highlands. After only about half an hour drive the driver pulled into a café and motioned that we were going to stop for half an hour to eat and rest. Murmuring began in the bus amongst the tourists. One young woman complained that she was told that we would be in Da Lat by 11:30. No way. The driver wanted everyone to get off the bus and eat and no one moved. We were at an impasse and mutiny was in the making. Someone needed to take charge and make a decision. I did. I stood up in the front of the bus and announced to everyone that I had traveled this road many times in the past and that the road ahead was curvy and dangerous and if the driver needed to stop for food and rest and smoke then we were stopping. If he felt comfortable continuing to drive then we would go on. The decision would ultimately be up to the driver. Thinh relayed this speech to the driver and he agreed to continue driving. Mutiny quelled.

The problem we had here was the fact that Westerners think time is perfect. Yes, in the West time is perfect, moving along at the rhythmic pace of tick, tock, tick, tock. But this is Viet Nam. Time moves differently here. It moves in fits of lurches and leaps and jumps with long pauses between. There is no predictability to these movements and non-movements. Time is the master of its own destiny. Man does not influence it by impatience or hurry or laziness or indifference. It moves as it will. Just throw your watch away and enjoy the trip! After I sat down from my bus speech one of the travelers, a girl with a wholesome girl-next-door look, asked me if I was hungry because she perceived that I would rather have stopped. I answered "I'm never hungry. I'm always hungry. You can eat anytime. Just enjoy the ride." She smiled with understanding and sat back to do just that.

Da Lat is the San Francisco of Viet Nam. It isn't on the seacoast but there is a lake at the base of the city. The city climbs up from the lake all around into many hills and valleys and ridges and canyons. Houses are built on the steep sides of every available space in the city. Where there is no house there are gardens, both commercial and private. The weather is cool and refreshing and a welcome relief from the swelter that is Sai Gon. But it's the night market that attracts the masses to this idyllic corner of paradise. Every night the center of town comes alive with the lights and sounds and movement of commerce. The ethnic people come in out of the hills to sell their needlework handicrafts and their produce and to shop for their own needs. They spread a cloth out on the sidewalk to display their wares in front of the passing shoppers. A family of four or five will pile onto their Honda for the trip to town for an evening of adventure. The allure of the city draws them in. The allure is universal!

We ate at a small café on a back street that serves only chicken and noodles in several different forms. I was the only foreigner amongst ethnic and Vietnamese diners. (This is the case most of the time here. I can be in the middle of a tourist attraction and, thanks to Thinh and Be, I will be taken to the spots where only the Vietnamese go and we will shun the tourist hang-outs. Thinh and Be present to me the REAL Viet Nam which the tourists miss. Lucky me. Unlucky them.[1]) After dinner I asked for something sweet so we walked to a pastry shop and took some dessert delights with us to the edge of the lake and ate sweet things under the black sky with its crescent moon and the lights of the market glowing under it all. We finished our dessert and went to an outdoor café that served only hot soy milk, hot bean milk and hot peanut milk. Be ordered our drinks and they arrived with steam billowing like nuke plant cooling towers. We piled spoonfuls of sugar into the drink and

---

1.) I have taken a lot of flack for this sentence from Vietnamese people. I'm thinking it's a language misunderstanding. I mean it's lucky for ME to go to these obscure places and unlucky for the REGULAR TOURISTS who miss them.

drank with care to avoid burning our tongues. Once again, I was the only white boy. Lucky me. Unlucky them. (see footnote)

The next day we caught the bus back to Sai Gon to reluctantly finish our four day rest-journey. The attendant walked the isle and collected tickets, handed out bottles of water and then passed out barf bags. This is not a good sign! Perhaps we have shipped out on Wolf Larsen's hell-ship GHOST. With any luck at all "We'll all win back to San Francisco." (Jack London) The road down the hill passes some of the richest agriculture land on earth and past the herds of hump-backed, red cattle and the occasional grey water buffalo with their sad-eyes and under turned horns that are so often the theme of Vietnamese art and craft. The coffee plantations of Bao Loc spread before us like a table cloth of rich green over the rolling hills as far as the eye could see and then we plunged down into the Dong Nai River basin over the steep and curvy descent that warranted the use of the barf bags. Passing over the bridge on the Dong Nai we discovered the fish farmers with their floating houses and their watery "farms" for front yards. Finally we came to the main Ha Noi/Ho Chi Minh City highway where the rubber trees grow, planted by the French decades ago. We turned south toward Sai Gon.

All the while on the bus ride the radio had been softly playing Vietnamese music, mostly sad and lonely "torch" songs with plaintiff electric guitars. In a land that has been dealt more than its fair share of weeping, the electric guitar players have mastered the art of making their instruments weep.

Ho Chi Minh City, Viet Nam
October 30, 2006

the play

A one act play based on Jesus' parable of the good Samaritan.
Luke 10:30-37

(Thank you Karla Lingren for rescuing this document from a crashed hard drive!)

the samaritan of metropolis
A One Act Play

The characters in order of appearance:

Old man
Hooligan
Skater Dude
Teenaged girl
Stock broker
Gay guy
Clinic nurse
Narrator off stage

Note: The director and actors have license to depict the characters using stereotyped clothes, mannerisms, speech patterns, and voice inflections to render the characters believable members of their particular subcultures.

The Act

Sub scene 1:

The stage is back dropped with a row-house scene from a residential street in a modern city in the U.S. with a sidewalk foreground. A neat, casually dressed o1d man enters stage left walking down the sidewalk as a shabby hooligan youth enters stage right walking toward the old man. When the two meet in the center, the youth attacks the old man and beats him and steals his wallet and runs off stage left leaving the old man lying, wounded against the row house back drop on the sidewalk. The only sounds are of the scuffle itself and the cries for help from the old man. He moans periodically through the next three sub-scenes.

Sub-scene 2:

A skater dude enters stage left walking down the sidewalk talking on a cell phone, a skateboard under his arm.

SKATER: Hey, Man! Did you catch the movie, The Fast and the Furious? Lots of fights and crashes...(His eyes meet the old man.)..Aawwh radical dude! (turns away.) I just saw one of the victims, dude. Lots of blood and bruises man. Or maybe he fell off his board. Wipe-out! I mean he bit the bullet bad. Man some of these skater dudes are really getting old. They don't even know how to skate anymore. That's such a drag, man. Oh well, that's his bad not ours. (Laughing) (His voice fades as he exits stage right.)

Sub-scene 3:

A teenaged girl enters stage right walking down the sidewalk talking on a cell phone, vigorously chewing gum.

GIRL: Like ahh whatever you know actua11y there's a sale at the mall today on dresses...(Her eyes meet the old man.)...AAWK! OOH, GAG ME! (Turns away.) Staci, these like homeless are getting so like loserville more and more tacky! They like sleep all day on the sidewalk and they like smell and this one like barfed all over himself. EEEEWW That was soooo last year. As if like how can these homeless people even stand themselves. (Her voice fades as she exits stage left.)

Sub-scene 4:

A three-piece-suited-yuppie-type thirties male carrying an attache case enters stage left and walks down the sidewalk talking on a cell phone.

BROKER: AT&T, yes AT&T. It's hit bottom and only has one way to go. It's time to move. (His eyes meet the old man's.) That reminds me. (Turns away.) Healthcare. There's a new healthcare company that'll I.P.O. this week and I think you should get in on the ground floor of this one. There's a lot of people in this country who need healthcare and you can make a lot of money on it. (His voice fades as he exits stage right.)

Sub-scene 5:

A gay guy enters stage left walking down the sidewalk talking on a cell phone.

GUY: Oh, we had a marvelous time last night...(His eyes meet the old man.)...OH MY GAWD!! My dear man! (with excitement and passion) What has happened to you! OH MY GAWD! Let me help you. Oh, you poor man. You're bleeding! (Screams.) Someone call 911! (In his excitement forgetting he has a phone.) There's a clinic right here down the street. Let me help you there. (He helps the old man up and half carries him a few doors down the sidewalk to

a nurse who has discreetly entered stage right.)
Nurse, please help us. This poor old man has
been attacked and beaten and robbed. He's
injured and bleeding. Please help him. (Still very
excited.) (They lay him down and the nurse
begins to tend to the old man.) (To the nurse.)
Here's a hundred dollars and my credit card.
Please care for him tonight and I'll return
tomorrow and pay you whatever you need. (To
the old man.) Oh, you poor man. Don't worry,
you're going to be all right.

NARRATOR OFF STAGE:

"Which of these...do you think proved to be a
neighbor to the man who fell into the robbers'
hands." Luke 10:36

Who is your Samaritan?

Curtain

sundries

preface to sundries

Following are short vignettes about "events" along the way. Life happens and here are some illustrations.

the café racer

My long time friend Gene Graf sent me a photo
essay of Rome the other day and the first few
photos were of the Coliseum. Immediately my
memory was flooded with my own picture essay
of Rome. Pam and I spent the year of 1971
traveling Europe on a 500cc Earles forked BMW,
living in a 6'X6' pup tent, sleeping in a sleeping
bag we had fashioned by sewing two together,
feeding ourselves over a tiny propane GAZ camp
stove with one cooking pot and seeing the world
with wide open eyes. The three most memorable
sites of the year were Stonehenge in England,
the Parthenon in Athens and the Coliseum in
Rome.

Rome was magic! We wandered the Coliseum
alone. (It seemed everywhere we went that year
it was "off season" and there were few other
tourists.) We walked with the ghosts of centuries
past...the gladiators, the Christians, the lions, the
slaves, commoners and kings. We imagined the
grandeur that once was and wondered at the ruin
that was now.

We stayed in the campground outside the city
and rode in during the day to see the sites. The
streets were jammed with tiny Fiat 500's with no
regard for lanes or deference. It was everyone
for themselves. It was Rome where we were
introduced to the Café racer.

One day we were stopped at a red light in the traffic circle surrounding the Coliseum and two boys rode up on either side of us on 500 triple Kawasakis. The bikes were stripped down to bare bones with clip-on bars and painted flat black and had the telltale scars of being dropped a few too many times. The late 60's and early 70's saw the emergence of the Super Bike and the triple Kawasaki was one of the fastest. (Nicknamed the "Widowmaker" due to its poor handling.) The machine was distinctive because of the exhaust system's twin pipes on the right side and single pipe on the other. It was a two cycle and under full throttle it looked like mosquito abatement. The boys beckoned us to follow them and they raced ahead, smoke in pursuit, and as they threw their heads back in uncontrolled joy their long hair flowed in their wake like the long tail of a dragon kite. We chased as best we could and they graciously waited for us at the next red light, laughing, and we all three raced off again at the green, stopped again at the next red and raced off again. We raced past 2,000 year old ruins on our 20th Century rockets. We did this for an hour or so and finally the boys disappeared into the traffic and we never saw them again. We were the triumphant gladiators of the New Rome. The city streets were our playground! The Café racer was our toy.

Carmichael California
September 2010

ode to rolley

Dale Earnhardt died yesterday, too. Now it's not that I still follow racing, especially the circle track stuff, but when a racer dies all racers weep. When it happens these days I'm amazed because racing is so much safer than it was years ago. I saw so many of my peers die back then but never gave it a thought. You couldn't and keep racing. After all, it was like Dan Gurney said "Racing is where you drive as fast as you can without killing yourself." Dale drove too fast yesterday.

I say "Dale Earnhardt died yesterday, TOO." because it feels like Rolley Miller died yesterday...and his wife...and his daughter. Pam and I have been moping around today like a friend died...yesterday. I'm sad but I'm angry, too. I'm angry at Rolley. I'm angry at his supporters. I'm angry at his detractors. ...I'm angry at myself. Why do people act like this?

Rolley was a good man. Imperfect, but good. He always preached the truth. I never caught him in a heresy. He was educated and well trained and had a heart for God. He was young and energetic and enthusiastic. He was compassionate. He was sincere. Now... he's gone.

We're becoming old hands at this now. It's the third for us. But we won't get used to it.

"They shoot their wounded don't they?" (O. Easterly)

relieved

Some time ago I developed what I thought was a cyst on the back side of my left shoulder. The doc looked at it and confirmed that it was a cyst and there was no need to remove it and not to worry about it. This week I finally found out what it REALLY is. You see, at some time in my past (and, of course, we never know when it is because we never remember these events, as I'm sure you already know) I was abducted by aliens. (Now, every time I tell this story to people many of them will start laughing at this point but as my dear friend I know you're not laughing now. You know this is serious business and you wouldn't laugh at a good friend of yours who had experienced it. So, for this obvious respect for my integrity I appreciate you.) Anyway, I was abducted by aliens and this so called "cyst" is a tracking devise they implanted in my body in order to monitor my movements. Isn't that wild?! It really all makes perfect sense to me now since I've been suspicious of this for a long time. Often when I'm facing North by Northwest with my mouth open I can hear this ringing in my head like the sounds of that L.A. County Boy's Choir, you know, that high pitched, multi-frequency, harmonic ringing that's not necessarily annoying but quite a distraction to normal conversation. This ringing and, of course, my fear of driving in the desert have lead me to believe that I've had "contact" and now I know it's true after learning about the implant. It's really quite a relief to know this, to have the mystery solved. Of course, I'm sure you already know, because you're so well read and intelligent that I CAN'T have it removed. They somehow have the devise connected to our health. If it's removed our health declines and we become useless and maybe even die. So I'll just merrily go along here with my tracking devise implant, adding to the knowledge base of some other-world data collection geek. Ain't science wonderful?

the drive home

The pre-planning paid off. It was a good week...a record. Of course, it was Valentine's week and that was to be expected. None the less, the reward from a successful venture was sweet even though the reward was fraught with exhaustion. I could unload this afternoon and go home tonight but was the risk of exhaustion-driving worth it? No, I'll head over to Felipe's and eat too much Mexican and drink too much wine and sleep good tonight and go home tomorrow. Buenos nochos Felipe's!

After a leisurely unloading of the truck and cleaning up of many details it was North to Oregon. Up I-5 and East on 20 to Clear Lake I repeated the drive home like a Canadian goose instinctively returning North after winter. The sun was setting over Clear Lake as I arrived and the reflection on the lake flashed the last light of a clear day to signal a starry night. By the time I reached 101 it was dark and the next six hours would be night driving. I like the night driving. Most of the amateurs are off the road and only the truck drivers remain. There's still a few drunks to contend with but they can be out during the day too.

The greatest hazard in night driving in this part of the country is the deer and elk, especially in the evening and morning hours. I've already hit two deer, one with my last truck and one with this one. The one with this one is still memorable. I didn't see the ill fated deer until he was right in front of my left headlight and then I only saw his terrified, bugged out eyes looking up into my lights just before the impact. The damage to my truck was regrettable but the damage to the deer was permanent. When I night-drive I always keep the memory of those terrified eyes in mind as I race through the ink-night with only the meager piercing of my halogens as guidance.

In January there had been an earthquake off the coast of Eureka damaging the road around Standish-Hickey. This is a fragile place anyway. The road or the mountain is always falling down from too much rain or just the natural "settling" of the Coast Range so it doesn't take much shaking to precipitate a slide. Coming down this month there were about one hour delays as repairs were being made so I expected the same heading home. I wasn't disappointed. Flashing out of the ink-night came the amber warning sign of "Road Work Ahead". I stopped behind the last car in line and shut down to wait. Rolling the window down I looked out into the night sky to witness a starry display numbering greater than Abram's descendants. The familiar Seven Sisters greeted me and Orion was still on sentry duty after all these years from learning about him as a Boy Scout. Now I have to take their word for it that there are seven in the Seven Sisters.

The darkness was interrupted by the oncoming line of traffic and then a time of darkness again and then our turn to go. The horizon began to glow as the light from the construction overcame the ink-night. Finally the rounding of the next curve revealed the project...man against nature. The mountain on the right had fallen on the roadway and the material was being removed and the cavity in the mountain was being filled like a decayed tooth. The filling was almost complete and was being covered with straw and net to hold the sown seeds of earth-holding grass to slow the coming of the next slide. Looking up the side of the mountain the D-8's looked like Tonkas and the men like ants.

On the left the road itself had fallen away and was being reenforced with piling and concrete. A huge crane was being used to drive and set the piling. When I came down the crane was erect and in the process of driving and setting but now, going back, it had been lowered to flat on the ground like a defeated Imperial Snow Walker. Men were scrabbling all over the triangulated framework of the crane like Lilliputians scrambling over a slumbering Gulliver as they re-rigged it for another attach on the mountainside. I think the mountain is winning.

Seeing the Tonka-Cats and the Liliputian-men under the expanse of the endless sky-dome, inlaid with its diamond-stars, drove home to me the smallness of man and the wonder of what this small creature has done here subduing the land. I can only hope this is what He had in mind.

Sacramento, California
March 7, 2001

the gorging

The surface of the water marked the demarcation between the two worlds. The watery world below boiled with the schools of anchovies while the airy world above boiled with the flocks of sea gulls. Amidst the two worlds were the seals going between the two as if owners of both. The hungry fog crouched in the distance like a waiting tiger. The scene was filled with the sounds of the squawking gulls and the barking seals and accompanied by the gently crashing surf. The gulls swooped down on the anchovy feast, filling their bellies to capacity. The seals "stood on their heads" in the water with their tails sticking straight up into the air like a Churchill victory "V" and then emerged upright with triumphant barking.

We watched the feeding from the shore having just left a feast of our own at The Prime. Our fare was also seafood with cod and prawn and scallop accented with beef and vegetables and pasta and undefined seasonings. We washed it down with whisky and wine and finished with chocolate cake so rich Marie Antoinette would blush.

The fog crept in for its fill of land. All varieties of things participated in the gorging.

Brookings, Oregon
May 27, 2001

the pick up

I bought Pamela a minivan yesterday. She has more delinquents than car to haul them in now so a van became a necessity. It's a first generation Toyota minivan from the '80's. It's one of those that look like a bullet on wheels or maybe a shoe on roller skates. It's funny looking. I still haven't mastered the art of entering the driver' seat. I've entered head first, feet first, butt first. I've dived in, crawled in, oozed in. Nothing works. Once in, it fits like a glove, or maybe a coffin. Anyhow, I bought the thing in Burlingame and needed to figure out how to pick it up from Sac. When I went to see it, I crossed a train track upon entering Burlingame and just at that moment a Cal Train passed. That's it. I'll take Greyhound to San Francisco and the train down the peninsula to Burlingame and walk to the van which I parked on the street after making the deal. It'll be an adventure, a public transportation adventure. Bilbo would be proud.

When I got back to Sac it was too late to call Nhuan for a ride to the station in the morning. I knew he worked somewhere downtown and thought I could get a lift from him on his way to work so I got up at 4:30 and booked over to his house to wait in the street until lights came on in the living room. I explained my "Toyota retrieval plan" to him and he graciously offered to give me a ride into town. It was still dark as I bid Nhuan goodbye and "wish me luck" and bought my one way to the city. The next bus left in five minutes. Now I hadn't been on the dog in many years but I knew this was going to be an interesting experience from a sociological perspective. After entering the bus, I wasn't disappointed. I looked down the aisle and each pair of seats on both sides of the bus were occupied by only one person. Of course, we're all strangers here and noone wants to sit next to a stranger so I worked my way to the back to find my own pair of unoccupied seats. There they were at the very back. I began to sit down to realize the aisle seat contained a pool of fresh blood, probably overflow from a super saturated Kotex or none at all. I chose the window seat and ignored the evidence of the previous occupant in the aisle seat.

Valerie came on the P.A. and announced she was our driver today (women do everything these days). She told us we couldn't smoke or cuss and there was a bathroom in the back. After her admonitions she eased the bus out into the street and the adventure began. Now, you know I burn up Interstate 80. I've got grooves worn in that road. I don't even need to steer. The truck just drives itself. But that cool, spring morning, with dawn just breaking over the snow capped Sierras, I-80 was a virgin highway to me. For one thing, I wasn't driving. I could look at things and not have to keep my eyes on the road. Also, the seats in the bus were higher off the ground than in my truck so I had a new perspective. Crossing over the river I could see East to the baseball field in West Sac and the Aztec pyramid building and West down the river to the marinas. The fields were green and stretched to the horizon with their bounties of rice and vegetables.

After the newness of the landscape wore off I began to peruse my travel mates and the interior of our transport. The first thing I noticed was a variety of aromas. Aromas? It smelled more like an NBA locker room after a playoff game. The aisles and the seats and the overhead bins all seemed to be carrying a lot of refuse from previous passengers...soda bottles and snack food wrappers and general debris. Most of the passengers looked like they had just stepped out of a Tom Waits song. Now, how can I put this, without being unkind or arrogant. Let me just say that most of them looked like they had made some choices in their individual histories that were not in their best interest. Well, we all make mistakes. I didn't feel completely out of place.

Because it was early morning it was quiet and peaceful in the bus and even comfortable. It was fast too. We zipped in the left lane passing almost everything and when the diamond lane appeared, it was ours. We approached Oakland for a quick stop. I couldn't help but think how disappointed Jack London would be to see how his town had deteriorated. But then, maybe Jack's not looking too good these days either. Most of my mates got off in Oakland and only about half a dozen remained for the trip over the bridge into SF. The city loomed clear and crisp across the bay. We passed over a super tanker on her way back to Alaska after having delivered her life blood for our nations economy. The bus lane took us right into the heart of the city and we all emerged into the bustle. I asked directions to the Cal Train station and headed off on foot for the couple mile city-hike passing Chinese speaking workers on the street with all of there sh-sh sounds in their language and each smoking a cigarette. I knew I was close to the station about two blocks from it as the passerby on the side walk began to look like attache-cased commuters. Sure enough, there it was, 4th and Townsend. I found the map, bought my ticket, and headed for Train 40 to San Jose.

The first car was the "bike" car, for those traveling with bicycles. There were wide bays to park the bikes and only a few seats to sit. I entered the second car which was for passengers. Like the bus, the double seats were occupied by only one passenger. The first thing that caught my attention was the personalized, melodic ring of a cell phone. I found a seat and immediately noticed that the caliber of the clientele had ratcheted up a notch or three. The baseball caps on backwards and the mushroom cuts and the rucksacks of the bus were replaced by the same baseball caps only on front wards and nylon and velcro laptop cases. There was a Japanese woman in the seat in front of me reading a Japanese fashion magazine who looked so elegant that I would have expected her to be chauffeured in a limo to San Jose rather than riding the commuter train. There was a grand fatherly black man sitting across the aisle from me with a fiercely protruding lower lip like Bubba in "Forrest Gump"...a fiercely protruding lower lip and a kind face. He, also, was dressed impeccably. In front of him was the business man who had taken the cell call and he seemed to be reading an order, either giving or taking, I couldn't tell. The conductor came by to punch our tickets and silently scolded the man and motioned him to turn it off. Let me just say that these people had probably made much better choices in their individual histories. I almost felt like the riffraff.

The train began to roll and the driver greeted us with his own admonitions quite similar to Valerie's. He said "Keep your feet on the floor. Get your feet off the seats and put them on the floor." He sounded like Miss Purdle's evil twin. (You remember Miss Purdle don't you?) Each stop had its bicycle commuters with their goofy pointed-in-the-rear helmets. Now come on, at the speeds these bicyclists travel do you really think they need that streamlined point-in-the-rear of their helmet? Now, I'm all for safety but I'd rather smash my noggin on the sidewalk and have my brains run into the gutter than wear one of those Duffus-looking helmets. The price of fashion is too high for me.

Now I come to the part that inspired me to tell you this story at all. One day, Loren was showing me photos of his most recent trip to India and in several street scenes there were box-looking affaires on the side walks. Loren said, "People live in those!" Of course this was no surprise to me after having seen similar poverty in Viet Nam, Latin America and Europe. It's the nature of poverty for people to live under marginal circumstances. Trains travel different routes than the roadways and sidewalks of a country. You get a different perspective on the city from the train than you do from the road, much like my different perspective on the bus. As the Cal Train moved South out of San Francisco we passed by little shanty towns beside the tracks where people had stretched blue tarps up to provide shelter and, of course, the ubiquitous boxes of make-shift housing. Loren's words reverberated in my ears, "People live in those!" and I said almost out loud "Here too". And Jesus said "For the poor you have with you always..." even in the greatest country this planet has ever seen.

March 20, 2002
Brookings, Oregon

it's a guzmania! (A collecting expedition in the rainforest of Ecuador.)

It's at least 98 degrees and 98 percent humidity. The equatorial sun beats down with relentless fury. You are sweating profusely as you trudge through the forest, your body aching from impossible hikes and endless hours in rickety jeeps over rutted roads. A purple headed Chimborazo hummingbird buzzes overhead and then launches straight up into the forest canopy as if to mock your earth bound existence. You feel a fever coming on and begin longing for the stiff cot in the primitive hotel room tonight. The rapping of the rain on the corrugated metal roof will audibly massage your wounded body and the strum of nylon string guitars downstairs will audibly massage your wounded mind. You just sank up to your knees in some hidden muck in the brush as you carve your way through the undergrowth with your faithful machete, desperately hoping that the deadly Fer-de-Lance pit viper is fast asleep over that next hill. Alas, another slash of vegetation (that will be grown back before you clear customs in Miami next week) reveals a dazzling array of red floral bracts atop burgundy-green foliage. It's a Guzmania! It's all been worth it!

The Guzmanias are the darlings of the Bromeliad hybridizers.The hybrids in commercial cultivation today are the result of decades of work and experimentation by a handful of dedicated growers in Holland, Belgium, Germany and the U.S. Bringing a Guzmania, or for that matter any Bromeliad into your home, is to experience a little of the tropical rain forest without destroying any of it or even working up a sweat. You can fantasize about sitting in a sidewalk café in Quito, a cool breeze caressing the nape of your neck, sipping Fanta while discussing the day's discovery which may become the parent of an award winning hybrid at the next Bromeliad World Conference.

Cheated the Fer-de-Lance again!

the tree house

It all started with a honey-do. Pam wanted the curly willow in the front yard pruned so the sidewalk would be passable. The day finally came when the nagging overpowered the procrastination. "Okay, you point, I'll cut." After about an hour of sawing and lopping and trimming and hauling and sweating the tree was pretty well cleaned out. I stood at the bottom of the tree and looked up at the space in the middle between the spreading branches and realized it was calling out to me for a tree house. The boys have been bugging us for a tree house for years but we didn't have a tree big enough to support one--until now.

The next weekend the three of use headed for the willow tree to build a tree house. In inventory I had a four foot by four foot piece of plywood that was framed with two-by-fours that I had used as a shelf in the mini van and that would make a perfect floor/platform. I also had many feet of mahogany one-by-six that I had removed from my new truck before outfitting it with new shelving. My intention was to secure the plywood platform and then erect two courses of one-by-six on edge to give a small stub wall around the platform. I visualized two two-by-fours running up to the platform from the lower branches with several one-by-four cross pieces for ladder steps. I wanted the platform and ladder to be as concealed as much as possible from the ground and street so to begin climbing the ladder you had to first climb the tree. (This would keep the pansies out!)

We hauled the framed plywood soon-to-be-floor out to the tree and the three of us pushed it up into the crotch of the spreading branches. Then I had to climb up under it and push it up further in the tree myself. There really wasn't room for the boys too so I had to do it alone and the sucker was heavy! I struggled and pushed and heaved and grunted and, of course, more sweating. I looked down at the boys one time when I stopped to rest and they were gawking up in silent, stunned amazement. Then Joel, with a furrowed brow of concern said, "Grandpa, are you all right? I don't want to lose the only bread winner for the family." Oh, thanks for the vote of confidence! The thing was more awkward than heavy though and I finally got it where I wanted it with one side fairly level by eye. I asked for the level to be handed up and leveled that one side and attached two screws to the tree to temporarily hold it. I then pushed the other side up level and secured it as well. We then cut two pieces of one-by-six to screw to the tree under the platform to provide a permanent resting place for the platform. The "foundation" for the platform was now in place and I screwed it securely to the tree and every place that the plywood or the two-by-four frame came in contact with a branch I put more screws. Finally it was solid and safe. We had a level platform.

Next we needed the ladder. I eyeballed where the two-by-fours should go and screwed them to the platform and the branches below creating two almost parallel verticals for the ladder and then attached the one-by-four cross pieces completing the access ladder. We could now climb the ladder and sit on the platform. All of the aforementioned work was done with me up in the tree barking down orders in my usual Captain Ahab style and the boys handing me up tools and materials as needed and offering critical advise and encouragement. As the platform and ladder took shape Matthew began to say he was going to be the first one up the ladder to sit on the platform so when the ladder was completed I told him to go up. He climbed the tree to the base of the ladder and hoisted himself up to the bottom rung and climbed the rungs to the platform and he was on, laughing and cheering about his new tree house.

Joel was next. He climbed up the tree to the lower rung on the ladder and stalled out. I won't say he had a fearful look on his face but more a look of bewilderment or dismay. I asked him if he was afraid to climb over to the ladder or did he just not know how to get there. (Remember, we wanted it to be difficult just to get to the ladder so we could keep the faint of heart out. This is man's territory!) He looked at me with his doe eyes and said, "Both". Okay, I told him where to climb and how to get to the ladder and then told him I was right below him and wouldn't let him fall. "Just climb it." He overcame his hesitation and climbed the tree to the ladder and then the ladder to the platform. Success! I then climbed up there with them and the three of us sat on the platform to peruse our labors. We were all a little nervous that there were no sides to keep a body from falling off the edge. It became apparent that the stub walls I had planned were very necessary.

We went back to work erecting the stub walls and finally our tree house was finished. Well, okay, it was really a tree 'platform' but at least a guy could climb up a tree and sit in relative comfort away from the world of deadlines and commitments and responsibilities and fantasize about what little boys fantasize about and be boys. They were happy. We called Grandma to come out and inspect our work which she did and even climbed the ladder to look in (she ain't no pansy!). We had her approval! The next day Matthew did his home work in the tree house and read his book.

The following week I visited one of my customers, Lisa and Jason at Kiyo's Florist. They have two sons the same age as Joel and Matthew so often times we exchanged boy stories while conducting business. When I told them about the tree house Jason recommended the movie "Sandlot" which is a baseball story but has a tree house in it. (Jason is one of those admirable fathers who is totally engaged with his boy's upbringing and they will turn out to be righteous and responsible adults in the midst of a decaying and corrupt culture.) Pam found the DVD for sale cheaper than we could rent it so she bought it and we all watched it together. The movie was a great recommendation with a sweet story but the tree house was a 'real' tree house. I mean it had walls and windows and roof and fireman's pole and rope ladder. The thing was deluxe. It put our primitive tree "platform" to shame. As soon as the movie was over it was "Pleeeeeze Grandpa, can we build walls and windows and a roof?" Rats! Thanks Jason!

The next weekend I told the boys I would exchange labor with them. "You help me unload the truck and I'll help you build a real house." So after church we did just that. We hauled out many lengths of the one-by-sixes and the tools and climbed up there and measured and sawed and screwed and hammered and, yes, sweated some more. Toward the end the boys started to lose interest, even though the house was shaping up nicely, so I asked what the problem was. Matthew said, "I'm tired and hungry and that's a bad combination with me." To which my reply was, "Me too, but let's finish the job. We're so close." So after the final course of one-by-six wall pieces was finished we went to the lumber inventory beside the house and found a four-by-eight sheet of plywood to cut in half for the roof. We carried it out to the front yard, cut it in half, and together we hoisted it up into the tree. The boys climbed up to the top of the house and in the branches and pulled while I pushed from below and finally, after much struggle (and sweat), the roof was in place. I climbed on top and fastened the final screws and it was done. We had a real tree house. Grandma came out to inspect and approve and we all ate dinner and went to bed tired but satisfied.

Tomorrow, when they're in school, I'm going out there and climb up in the tree house and be ten again.

September, 2010
Carmichael, California

about the author

Ron Callison is an entrepreneur in the horticulture industry in California doing business as Treeborne Gardens Worldwide, Inc. <Treeborn.com> His travels associated with the business have included South America, Europe and Asia. In 1994 he established a Bromeliad nursery in Viet Nam, introducing the country to this family of plants. The first story in **"the collection"** is from an adventure in Morocco during a year long motorcycle circuit in Europe in 1971. He also builds café racer motorcycles under the banner of ...rolls of thunder motowerks, inc. <RollsOfThunder.com>. Ron lives in Carmichael, California with Pamela, his wife of over 45 years, and their grandsons, Matthew and Joel.

"He hath shewed thee, O man, what is good; and what doth the Lord require of thee, **but to do justly, and to love mercy, and to walk humbly with thy God.**" Micah 6:8

Mango Moon Press, Inc.

"The melancholy mango moon hung low in the evening sky behind the blackened silhouette of the city scape." (anonymous)
Mango Moon Press publishes art books and other free wheeling, organic and home grown literature. Submissions accepted. E-mail <mangomoonpress@yahoo.com> or <info@mangomoonpress.com>

Made in the USA
Columbia, SC
31 August 2024

40830338R00095